THE 2014 SECONDARY NATIONAL CURRICULUM IN ENGLAND

KEY STAGES 3&4 FRAMEWORK DOCUMENT

To purchase a copy please visit:

www.thenationalcurriculum.com

or scan this code to take you there:

© Crown copyright 2013
Corporate Author: The Department For Education
Published by: Shurville Publishing

Contents

1. Introduction

1.1 This document sets out the framework for the national curriculum at key stages 3 and 4 and includes:

- contextual information about both the overall school curriculum and the statutory national curriculum, including the statutory basis of the latter

- aims for the statutory national curriculum

- statements on inclusion, and on the development of pupils' competence in numeracy and mathematics, language and literacy across the school curriculum

- programmes of study key stages 3 and 4 for all the national curriculum subjects, other than for key stage 4 English, mathematics and science, which will follow.

2. The school curriculum in England

2.1 Every state-funded school must offer a curriculum which is balanced and broadly based[1] and which:

- promotes the spiritual, moral, cultural, mental and physical development of pupils at the school and of society, and

- prepares pupils at the school for the opportunities, responsibilities and experiences of later life.

2.2 The school curriculum comprises all learning and other experiences that each school plans for its pupils. The national curriculum forms one part of the school curriculum.

2.3 All state schools are also required to make provision for a daily act of collective worship and must teach religious education to pupils at every key stage and sex and relationship education to pupils in secondary education.

2.4 Maintained schools in England are legally required to follow the statutory national curriculum which sets out in programmes of study, on the basis of key stages, subject content for those subjects that should be taught to all pupils. All schools must publish their school curriculum by subject and academic year online.[2]

2.5 All schools should make provision for personal, social, health and economic education (PSHE), drawing on good practice. Schools are also free to include other subjects or topics of their choice in planning and designing their own programme of education.

---

[1] See Section 78 of the 2002 Education Act: http://www.legislation.gov.uk/ukpga/2002/32/section/78 which applies to all maintained schools. Academies are also required to offer a broad and balanced curriculum in accordance with Section 1 of the 2010 Academies Act: http://www.legislation.gov.uk/ukpga/2010/32/section/1

[2] From September 2012, all schools are required to publish information in relation to each academic year, relating to the content of the school's curriculum for each subject and details about how additional information relating to the curriculum may be obtained: http://www.legislation.gov.uk/uksi/2012/1124/made

3. The national curriculum in England

Aims

3.1 The national curriculum provides pupils with an introduction to the essential knowledge that they need to be educated citizens. It introduces pupils to the best that has been thought and said; and helps engender an appreciation of human creativity and achievement.

3.2 The national curriculum is just one element in the education of every child. There is time and space in the school day and in each week, term and year to range beyond the national curriculum specifications. The national curriculum provides an outline of core knowledge around which teachers can develop exciting and stimulating lessons to promote the development of pupils' knowledge, understanding and skills as part of the wider school curriculum.

Structure

3.3 Pupils of compulsory school age in community and foundation schools, including community special schools and foundation special schools, and in voluntary aided and voluntary controlled schools, must follow the national curriculum. It is organised on the basis of four key stages and twelve subjects, classified in legal terms as 'core' and 'other foundation' subjects.

3.4 The Secretary of State for Education is required to publish programmes of study for each national curriculum subject, setting out the 'matters, skills and processes' to be taught at each key stage. Schools are free to choose how they organise their school day, as long as the content of the national curriculum programmes of study is taught to all pupils.

3.5   The structure of the national curriculum, in terms of which subjects are compulsory at each key stage, is set out in the table below:

Figure 1 – Structure of the national curriculum

	Key stage 1	Key stage 2	Key stage 3	Key stage 4
Age	5 – 7	7 – 11	11 – 14	14 – 16
Year groups	1 – 2	3 – 6	7 – 9	10 – 11
Core subjects				
English	✓	✓	✓	✓
Mathematics	✓	✓	✓	✓
Science	✓	✓	✓	✓
Foundation subjects				
Art and design	✓	✓	✓	
Citizenship			✓	✓
Computing	✓	✓	✓	✓
Design and technology	✓	✓	✓	
Languages[3]		✓	✓	
Geography	✓	✓	✓	
History	✓	✓	✓	
Music	✓	✓	✓	
Physical education	✓	✓	✓	✓

3.6   All schools are also required to teach religious education at all key stages. Secondary schools must provide sex and relationship education.

Figure 2 – Statutory teaching of religious education and sex and relationship education

	Key stage 1	Key stage 2	Key stage 3	Key stage 4
Age	5 – 7	7 – 11	11 – 14	14 – 16
Year groups	1 – 2	3 – 6	7 – 9	10 – 11
Religious education	✓	✓	✓	✓
Sex and relationship education			✓	✓

---

[3]   At key stage 2 the subject title is 'foreign language'; at key stage 3 it is 'modern foreign language'.

Key stage 4 entitlement areas

3.7 The arts (comprising art and design, music, dance, drama and media arts), design and technology, the humanities (comprising geography and history) and modern foreign language are not compulsory national curriculum subjects after the age of 14, but all pupils in maintained schools have a statutory entitlement to be able to study a subject in each of those four areas.

3.8 The statutory requirements in relation to the entitlement areas are:

- schools must provide access to a minimum of one course in each of the four entitlement areas

- schools must provide the opportunity for pupils to take a course in all four areas, should they wish to do so

- a course that meets the entitlement requirements must give pupils the opportunity to obtain an approved qualification.

4. Inclusion

Setting suitable challenges

4.1 Teachers should set high expectations for every pupil. They should plan stretching work for pupils whose attainment is significantly above the expected standard. They have an even greater obligation to plan lessons for pupils who have low levels of prior attainment or come from disadvantaged backgrounds. Teachers should use appropriate assessment to set targets which are deliberately ambitious.

Responding to pupils' needs and overcoming potential barriers for individuals and groups of pupils

4.2 Teachers should take account of their duties under equal opportunities legislation that covers race, disability, sex, religion or belief, sexual orientation, pregnancy and maternity, and gender reassignment.[4]

4.3 A wide range of pupils have special educational needs, many of whom also have disabilities. Lessons should be planned to ensure that there are no barriers to every pupil achieving. In many cases, such planning will mean that these pupils will be able to study the full national curriculum. The SEN Code of Practice includes advice on approaches to identification of need which can support this. A minority of pupils will need access to specialist equipment and different approaches. The SEN Code of Practice outlines what needs to be done for them.

4.4 With the right teaching, that recognises their individual needs, many disabled pupils may have little need for additional resources beyond the aids which they use as part of their daily life. Teachers must plan lessons so that these pupils can study every national curriculum subject. Potential areas of difficulty should be identified and addressed at the outset of work.

4.5 Teachers must also take account of the needs of pupils whose first language is not English. Monitoring of progress should take account of the pupil's age, length of time in this country, previous educational experience and ability in other languages.

4.6 The ability of pupils for whom English is an additional language to take part in the national curriculum may be in advance of their communication skills in English. Teachers should plan teaching opportunities to help pupils develop their English and should aim to provide the support pupils need to take part in all subjects.

---

[4] Age is a protected characteristic under the Equality Act 2010 but it is not applicable to schools in relation to education or (as far as relating to those under the age of 18) the provision of services; it is a relevant protected characteristic in relation to the provision of services or employment (so when thinking about staff). Marriage and civil partnership are also a protected characteristic but only in relation to employment.

5. Numeracy and mathematics

5.1   Teachers should use every relevant subject to develop pupils' mathematical fluency. Confidence in numeracy and other mathematical skills is a precondition of success across the national curriculum.

5.2   Teachers should develop pupils' numeracy and mathematical reasoning in all subjects so that they understand and appreciate the importance of mathematics. Pupils should be taught to apply arithmetic fluently to problems, understand and use measures, make estimates and sense check their work. Pupils should apply their geometric and algebraic understanding, and relate their understanding of probability to the notions of risk and uncertainty. They should also understand the cycle of collecting, presenting and analysing data. They should be taught to apply their mathematics to both routine and non-routine problems, including breaking down more complex problems into a series of simpler steps.

6. Language and literacy

6.1 Teachers should develop pupils' spoken language, reading, writing and vocabulary as integral aspects of the teaching of every subject. English is both a subject in its own right and the medium for teaching; for pupils, understanding the language provides access to the whole curriculum. Fluency in the English language is an essential foundation for success in all subjects.

Spoken language

6.2 Pupils should be taught to speak clearly and convey ideas confidently using Standard English. They should learn to justify ideas with reasons; ask questions to check understanding; develop vocabulary and build knowledge; negotiate; evaluate and build on the ideas of others; and select the appropriate register for effective communication. They should be taught to give well-structured descriptions and explanations and develop their understanding through speculating, hypothesising and exploring ideas. This will enable them to clarify their thinking as well as organise their ideas for writing.

Reading and writing

6.3 Teachers should develop pupils' reading and writing in all subjects to support their acquisition of knowledge. Pupils should be taught to read fluently, understand extended prose (both fiction and non-fiction) and be encouraged to read for pleasure. Schools should do everything to promote wider reading. They should provide library facilities and set ambitious expectations for reading at home. Pupils should develop the stamina and skills to write at length, with accurate spelling and punctuation. They should be taught the correct use of grammar. They should build on what they have been taught to expand the range of their writing and the variety of the grammar they use. The writing they do should include narratives, explanations, descriptions, comparisons, summaries and evaluations: such writing supports them in rehearsing, understanding and consolidating what they have heard or read.

Vocabulary development

6.4 Pupils' acquisition and command of vocabulary are key to their learning and progress across the whole curriculum. Teachers should therefore develop vocabulary actively, building systematically on pupils' current knowledge. They should increase pupils' store of words in general; simultaneously, they should also make links between known and new vocabulary and discuss the shades of meaning in similar words. In this way, pupils expand the vocabulary choices that are available to them when they write. In addition, it is vital for pupils' comprehension that they understand the meanings of words they meet in their reading across all subjects, and older pupils should be taught the meaning of instruction verbs that they may meet in examination questions. It is particularly important to induct pupils into the language which defines each subject in its own right, such as accurate mathematical and scientific language.

7. Programmes of study and attainment targets

7.1 The following pages set out the statutory programmes of study and attainment targets for key stages 3 and 4 for all subjects, except for English, mathematics and science at key stage 4. Schools are not required by law to teach the example content in [square brackets] or the content indicated as being 'non-statutory'.

English

Purpose of study

English has a pre-eminent place in education and in society. A high-quality education in English will teach pupils to speak and write fluently so that they can communicate their ideas and emotions to others and through their reading and listening, others can communicate with them. Through reading in particular, pupils have a chance to develop culturally, emotionally, intellectually, socially and spiritually. Literature, especially, plays a key role in such development. Reading also enables pupils both to acquire knowledge and to build on what they already know. All the skills of language are essential to participating fully as a member of society; pupils, therefore, who do not learn to speak, read and write fluently and confidently are effectively disenfranchised.

Aims

The overarching aim for English in the national curriculum is to promote high standards of language and literacy by equipping pupils with a strong command of the spoken and written word, and to develop their love of literature through widespread reading for enjoyment. The national curriculum for English aims to ensure that all pupils:

- read easily, fluently and with good understanding

- develop the habit of reading widely and often, for both pleasure and information

- acquire a wide vocabulary, an understanding of grammar and knowledge of linguistic conventions for reading, writing and spoken language

- appreciate our rich and varied literary heritage

- write clearly, accurately and coherently, adapting their language and style in and for a range of contexts, purposes and audiences

- use discussion in order to learn; they should be able to elaborate and explain clearly their understanding and ideas

- are competent in the arts of speaking and listening, making formal presentations, demonstrating to others and participating in debate.

Spoken language

The national curriculum for English reflects the importance of spoken language in pupils' development across the whole curriculum – cognitively, socially and linguistically. Spoken language continues to underpin the development of pupils' reading and writing during key stage 3 and teachers should therefore ensure pupils' confidence and competence in this area continue to develop. Pupils should be taught to understand and use the conventions for discussion and debate, as well as continuing to develop their skills in working collaboratively with their peers to discuss reading, writing and speech across the curriculum.

Reading and writing

Reading at key stage 3 should be wide, varied and challenging. Pupils should be expected to read whole books, to read in depth and to read for pleasure and information.

Pupils should continue to develop their knowledge of and skills in writing, refining their drafting skills and developing resilience to write at length. They should be taught to write formal and academic essays as well as writing imaginatively. They should be taught to write for a variety of purposes and audiences across a range of contexts. This requires an increasingly wide knowledge of vocabulary and grammar.

Opportunities for teachers to enhance pupils' vocabulary will arise naturally from their reading and writing. Teachers should show pupils how to understand the relationships between words, how to understand nuances in meaning, and how to develop their understanding of, and ability to use, figurative language.

Pupils should be taught to control their speaking and writing consciously, understand why sentences are constructed as they are and to use Standard English. They should understand and use age-appropriate vocabulary, including linguistic and literary terminology, for discussing their reading, writing and spoken language. This involves consolidation, practice and discussion of language. It is important that pupils learn the correct grammatical terms in English and that these terms are integrated within teaching.

Teachers should build on the knowledge and skills that pupils have been taught at key stage 2. Decisions about progression should be based on the security of pupils' linguistic knowledge, skills and understanding and their readiness to progress to the next stage. Pupils whose linguistic development is more advanced should be challenged through being offered opportunities for increased breadth and depth in reading and writing. Those who are less fluent should consolidate their knowledge, understanding and skills, including through additional practice.

Glossary

A non-statutory Glossary is provided for teachers.

Attainment targets

By the end of key stage 3, pupils are expected to know, apply and understand the matters, skills and processes specified in the relevant programme of study.

Key stage 3

Subject content

Reading

Pupils should be taught to:

- develop an appreciation and love of reading, and read increasingly challenging material independently through:

  - reading a wide range of fiction and non-fiction, including in particular whole books, short stories, poems and plays with a wide coverage of genres, historical periods, forms and authors. The range will include high-quality works from:

    - English literature, both pre-1914 and contemporary, including prose, poetry and drama
    - Shakespeare (two plays)
    - seminal world literature

  - choosing and reading books independently for challenge, interest and enjoyment.

  - re-reading books encountered earlier to increase familiarity with them and provide a basis for making comparisons.

- understand increasingly challenging texts through:

  - learning new vocabulary, relating it explicitly to known vocabulary and understanding it with the help of context and dictionaries

  - making inferences and referring to evidence in the text

  - knowing the purpose, audience for and context of the writing and drawing on this knowledge to support comprehension

  - checking their understanding to make sure that what they have read makes sense.

- read critically through:

  - knowing how language, including figurative language, vocabulary choice, grammar, text structure and organisational features, presents meaning

  - recognising a range of poetic conventions and understanding how these have been used

  - studying setting, plot, and characterisation, and the effects of these

  - understanding how the work of dramatists is communicated effectively through performance and how alternative staging allows for different interpretations of a play

  - making critical comparisons across texts

  - studying a range of authors, including at least two authors in depth each year.

Writing

Pupils should be taught to:

- write accurately, fluently, effectively and at length for pleasure and information through:
    - writing for a wide range of purposes and audiences, including:
        - well-structured formal expository and narrative essays
        - stories, scripts, poetry and other imaginative writing
        - notes and polished scripts for talks and presentations
        - a range of other narrative and non-narrative texts, including arguments, and personal and formal letters
    - summarising and organising material, and supporting ideas and arguments with any necessary factual detail
    - applying their growing knowledge of vocabulary, grammar and text structure to their writing and selecting the appropriate form
    - drawing on knowledge of literary and rhetorical devices from their reading and listening to enhance the impact of their writing
- plan, draft, edit and proof-read through:
    - considering how their writing reflects the audiences and purposes for which it was intended
    - amending the vocabulary, grammar and structure of their writing to improve its coherence and overall effectiveness
    - paying attention to accurate grammar, punctuation and spelling; applying the spelling patterns and rules set out in English Appendix 1 to the key stage 1 and 2 programmes of study for English.

Grammar and vocabulary

Pupils should be taught to:

- consolidate and build on their knowledge of grammar and vocabulary through:
    - extending and applying the grammatical knowledge set out in English Appendix 2 to the key stage 1 and 2 programmes of study to analyse more challenging texts
    - studying the effectiveness and impact of the grammatical features of the texts they read
    - drawing on new vocabulary and grammatical constructions from their reading and listening, and using these consciously in their writing and speech to achieve particular effects
    - knowing and understanding the differences between spoken and written language, including differences associated with formal and informal registers, and between Standard English and other varieties of English
    - using Standard English confidently in their own writing and speech

- discussing reading, writing and spoken language with precise and confident use of linguistic and literary terminology.[5]

Spoken English

Pupils should be taught to:

- speak confidently and effectively, including through:

    - using Standard English confidently in a range of formal and informal contexts, including classroom discussion

    - giving short speeches and presentations, expressing their own ideas and keeping to the point

    - participating in formal debates and structured discussions, summarising and/or building on what has been said

    - improvising, rehearsing and performing play scripts and poetry in order to generate language and discuss language use and meaning, using role, intonation, tone, volume, mood, silence, stillness and action to add impact.

---

[5] Teachers should refer to the Glossary that accompanies the programmes of study for English for their own information on the range of terms used within the programmes of study as a whole.

Glossary for the programmes of study for English (non-statutory)

The following glossary includes all the technical grammatical terms used in the programmes of study for English, as well as others that might be useful. It is intended as an aid for teachers, not as the body of knowledge that should be learnt by pupils. Apart from a few which are used only in schools (for example, *root word*), the terms below are used with the meanings defined here in most modern books on English grammar. It is recognised that there are different schools of thought on grammar, but the terms defined here clarify those being used in the programmes of study. For further details, teachers should consult the many books that are available.

Terms in definitions

As in any tightly structured area of knowledge, grammar, vocabulary and spelling involve a network of technical concepts that help to define each other. Consequently, the definition of one concept builds on other concepts that are equally technical. Concepts that are defined elsewhere in the glossary are hyperlinked. For some concepts, the technical definition may be slightly different from the meaning that some teachers may have learnt at school or may have been using with their own pupils; in these cases, the more familiar meaning is also discussed.

Term	Guidance	Example
active voice	An active verb has its usual pattern of subject and object (in contract with the passive).	Active: *The school arranged a visit.* Passive: *A visit was arranged* by the school.
adjective	The surest way to identify adjectives is by the ways they can be used: ▪ before a noun, to make the noun's meaning more specific (i.e. to modify the noun), or ▪ after the verb *be*, as its complement. Adjectives cannot be modified by other adjectives. This distinguishes them from nouns, which can be. Adjectives are sometimes called 'describing words' because they pick out single characteristics such as size or colour. This is often true, but it doesn't help to distinguish adjectives from other word classes,	*The pupils did some really good work.* [adjective used before a noun, to modify it] *Their work was good.* [adjective used after the verb *be*, as its complement] Not adjectives: *The lamp glowed.* [verb] *It was such a bright red!* [noun] *He spoke loudly.* [adverb] *It was a French grammar book.* [noun]

Term	Guidance	Example
	because <u>verbs</u>, <u>nouns</u> and <u>adverbs</u> can do the same thing.	
adverb	The surest way to identify adverbs is by the ways they can be used: they can <u>modify</u> a <u>verb</u>, an <u>adjective</u>, another adverb or even a whole clause. Adverbs are sometimes said to describe manner or time. This is often true, but it doesn't help to distinguish adverbs from other word classes that can be used as <u>adverbials</u>, such as <u>preposition phrases</u>, <u>noun phrases</u> and <u>subordinate clauses</u>.	*Usha <u>soon</u> started snoring <u>loudly</u>.* [adverbs modifying the verbs *started* and *snoring*] *That match was <u>really</u> exciting!* [adverb modifying the adjective *exciting*] *We don't get to play games <u>very</u> often.* [adverb modifying the other adverb, *often*] *<u>Fortunately,</u> it didn't rain.* [adverb modifying the whole clause 'it didn't rain' by commenting on it] Not adverbs: ▪ *Usha went <u>up the stairs</u>.* [preposition phrase used as adverbial] ▪ *She finished her work <u>this evening</u>.* [noun phrase used as adverbial] ▪ *She finished <u>when the teacher got cross</u>.* [subordinate clause used as adverbial]
adverbial	An adverbial is a word or phrase that is used, like an adverb, to modify a verb or clause. Of course, <u>adverbs</u> can be used as adverbials, but many other types of words and phrases can be used this way, including <u>preposition phrases</u> and <u>subordinate clauses</u>.	The *bus leaves <u>in five minutes</u>.* [preposition phrase as adverbial: modifies *leaves*] *She promised to see him <u>last night</u>.* [noun phrase modifying either *promised* or *see*, according to the intended meaning] *She worked <u>until she had finished</u>.* [subordinate clause as adverbial]
antonym	Two words are antonyms if their meanings are opposites.	*hot – cold* *light – dark* *light – heavy*
apostrophe	Apostrophes have two completely different uses: ▪ showing the place of missing letters (e.g. *I'm* for *I am*)	*<u>I'm</u> going out and I <u>won't</u> be long.* [showing missing letters] *<u>Hannah's</u> mother went to town in <u>Justin's</u> car.* [marking possessives]

Term	Guidance	Example
	▪ marking possessives (e.g. *Hannah's mother*).	
article	The articles *the* (definite) and *a* or *an* (indefinite) are the most common type of determiner.	*The* dog found *a* bone in *an* old box.
auxiliary verb	The auxiliary verbs are: *be, have, do* and the modal verbs. They can be used to make questions and negative statements. In addition: ▪ *be* is used in the progressive and passive ▪ *have* is used in the perfect ▪ *do* is used to form questions and negative statements if no other auxiliary verb is present	*They are winning the match.* [*be* used in the progressive] *Have you finished your picture?* [*have* used to make a question, and the perfect] *No, I don't know him.* [*do* used to make a negative; no other auxiliary is present] *Will you come with me or not?* [modal verb *will* used to make a question about the other person's willingness]
clause	A clause is a special type of phrase whose head is a verb. Clauses can sometimes be complete sentences. Clauses may be main or subordinate. Traditionally, a clause had to have a finite verb, but most modern grammarians also recognise non-finite clauses.	*It was raining.* [single-clause sentence] *It was raining but we were indoors.* [two finite clauses] *If you are coming to the party, please let us know.* [finite subordinate clause inside a finite main clause] *Usha went upstairs to play on her computer.* [non-finite clause]
cohesion	A text has cohesion if it is clear how the meanings of its parts fit together. Cohesive devices can help to do this. In the example, there are repeated references to the same thing (shown by the different style pairings), and the logical relations, such as time and cause, between different parts are clear.	**A visit** has been arranged for *__Year 6__*, to the Mountain Peaks Field Study Centre, leaving school at 9.30am. **This** is **an overnight visit**. The centre has beautiful grounds and *a nature trail*. During the afternoon, *__the children__* will follow *the trail*.
cohesive device	Cohesive devices are words used to show how the different parts of a text fit together. In other words, they create cohesion.	*Julia's dad bought her a football. The football was expensive!* [determiner; refers us back to a particular football]

Term	Guidance	Example
	Some examples of cohesive devices are: • determiners and pronouns, which can refer back to earlier words • conjunctions and adverbs, which can make relations between words clear • ellipsis of expected words.	*Joe was given a bike for Christmas. He liked it very much.* [the pronouns refer back to Joe and the bike] *We'll be going shopping before we go to the park.* [conjunction; makes a relationship of time clear] *I'm afraid we're going to have to wait for the next train. Meanwhile, we could have a cup of tea.* [adverb; refers back to the time of waiting] *Where are you going? [_] To school!* [ellipsis of the expected words *I'm going*; links the answer back to the question]
complement	A verb's subject complement adds more information about its subject, and its object complement does the same for its object. Unlike the verb's object, its complement may be an adjective. The verb *be* normally has a complement.	*She is our teacher.* [adds more information about the subject, *she*] *They seem very competent.* [adds more information about the subject, *they*] *Learning makes me happy.* [adds more information about the object, *me*]
compound, compounding	A compound word contains at least two root words in its morphology; e.g. *whiteboard, superman.* Compounding is very important in English.	*blackbird, blow-dry, bookshop, ice-cream, English teacher, inkjet, one-eyed, bone-dry, baby-sit, daydream, outgrow*
conjunction	A conjunction links two words or phrases together. There are two main types of conjunctions: • co-ordinating conjunctions (e.g. *and*) link two words or phrases together as an equal pair • subordinating conjunctions (e.g. *when*) introduce a subordinate clause.	*James bought a bat and ball.* [links the words *bat* and *ball* as an equal pair] *Kylie is young but she can kick the ball hard.* [links two clauses as an equal pair] *Everyone watches when Kyle does back-flips.* [introduces a subordinate clause] *Joe can't practise kicking because he's injured.* [introduces a subordinate clause]

Term	Guidance	Example
consonant	A sound which is produced when the speaker closes off or obstructs the flow of air through the vocal tract, usually using lips, tongue or teeth. Most of the letters of the alphabet represent consonants. Only the letters *a, e, i, o, u* and *y* can represent vowel sounds.	/p/ [flow of air stopped by the lips, then released] /t/ [flow of air stopped by the tongue touching the roof of the mouth, then released] /f/ [flow of air obstructed by the bottom lip touching the top teeth] /s/ [flow of air obstructed by the tip of the tongue touching the gum line]
continuous	See progressive	
co-ordinate, co-ordination	Words or phrases are co-ordinated if they are linked as an equal pair by a co-ordinating conjunction (i.e. *and, but, or*). In the examples on the right, the co-ordinated elements are shown in bold, and the conjunction is underlined. The difference between co-ordination and subordination is that, in subordination, the two linked elements are not equal.	***Susan*** <u>*and*</u> ***Amra*** *met in a café.* [links the words *Susan* and *Amra* as an equal pair] ***They talked*** <u>*and*</u> ***drank tea*** *for an hour.* [links two clauses as an equal pair] ***Susan got a bus*** <u>*but*</u> ***Amra walked.*** [links two clauses as an equal pair] Not co-ordination: *They ate* <u>*before*</u> *they met.* [*before* introduces a subordinate clause]
determiner	A determiner specifies a noun as known or unknown, and it goes before any modifiers (e.g. adjectives or other nouns). Some examples of determiners are: ■ articles (*the, a* or *an*) ■ demonstratives (e.g. *this, those*) ■ possessives (e.g. *my, your*) ■ quantifiers (e.g. *some, every*).	<u>*the*</u> *home team* [article, specifies the team as known] <u>*a*</u> *good team* [article, specifies the team as unknown] <u>*that*</u> *pupil* [demonstrative, known] <u>*Julia's*</u> *parents* [possessive, known] <u>*some*</u> *big boys* [quantifier, unknown] Contrast: *home* <u>*the*</u> *team, big* <u>*some*</u> *boys* [both incorrect, because the determiner should come before other modifiers]
digraph	A type of grapheme where two letters represent one phoneme. Sometimes, these two letters are not next to one another; this is called a	The digraph *ea* in *each* is pronounced /iː/. The digraph *sh* in *shed* is pronounced /ʃ/.

Term	Guidance	Example
	split digraph.	The split digraph _i–e_ in _line_ is pronounced /aɪ/.
ellipsis	Ellipsis is the omission of a word or phrase which is expected and predictable.	_Frankie waved to Ivana and ~~she~~ watched her drive away._ _She did it because she wanted to ~~do it~~._
etymology	A word's etymology is its history: its origins in earlier forms of English or other languages, and how its form and meaning have changed. Many words in English have come from Greek, Latin or French.	The word _school_ was borrowed from a Greek word ό÷ïëÞ (_skholé_) meaning 'leisure'. The word _verb_ comes from Latin _verbum_, meaning 'word'. The word _mutton_ comes from French _mouton_, meaning 'sheep'.
finite verb	Every sentence typically has at least one verb which is either past or present tense. Such verbs are called 'finite'. The imperative verb in a command is also finite. Verbs that are not finite, such as participles or infinitives, cannot stand on their own: they are linked to another verb in the sentence.	_Lizzie does the dishes every day._ [present tense] _Even Hana did the dishes yesterday._ [past tense] _Do the dishes, Naser!_ [imperative] Not finite verbs: ▪ _I have done them._ [combined with the finite verb _have_] ▪ _I will do them._ [combined with the finite verb _will_] ▪ _I want to do them!_ [combined with the finite verb _want_]
fronting, fronted	A word or phrase that normally comes after the verb may be moved before the verb: when this happens, we say it has been 'fronted'. For example, a fronted adverbial is an adverbial which has been moved before the verb. When writing fronted phrases, we often follow them with a comma.	_Before we begin, make sure you've got a pencil._ [Without fronting: _Make sure you've got a pencil before we begin._] _The day after tomorrow, I'm visiting my granddad._ [Without fronting: _I'm visiting my granddad the day after tomorrow._]
future	Reference to future time can be marked in a number of different ways in English. All these ways involve the use of a present-tense verb. See also tense. Unlike many other languages (such	_He will leave tomorrow._ [present-tense _will_ followed by infinitive _leave_] _He may leave tomorrow._ [present-tense _may_ followed by infinitive _leave_]

Term	Guidance	Example
	as French, Spanish or Italian), English has no distinct 'future tense' form of the verb comparable with its present and past tenses.	*He leaves tomorrow.* [present-tense *leaves*] *He is going to leave tomorrow.* [present tense *is* followed by *going to* plus the infinitive *leave*]
GPC	See grapheme-phoneme correspondences.	
grapheme	A letter, or combination of letters, that corresponds to a single phoneme within a word.	The grapheme *t* in the words *ten*, *bet* and *ate* corresponds to the phoneme /t/. The grapheme *ph* in the word *dolphin* corresponds to the phoneme /f/.
grapheme-phoneme correspondences	The links between letters, or combinations of letters (graphemes) and the speech sounds (phonemes) that they represent. In the English writing system, graphemes may correspond to different phonemes in different words.	The grapheme *s* corresponds to the phoneme /s/ in the word *see*, but… …it corresponds to the phoneme /z/ in the word *easy*.
head	See phrase.	
homonym	Two different words are homonyms if they both look exactly the same when written, and sound exactly the same when pronounced.	*Has he left yet? Yes – he went through tho door on tho loft.* *The noise a dog makes is called a bark. Trees have bark.*
homophone	Two different words are homophones if they sound exactly the same when pronounced.	*hear, here* *some, sum*
infinitive	A verb's infinitive is the basic form used as the head-word in a dictionary (e.g. *walk, be*). Infinitives are often used: ▪ after *to* ▪ after modal verbs.	*I want to walk.* *I will be quiet.*
inflection	When we add *-ed* to *walk*, or change *mouse* to *mice*, this change of morphology produces an inflection ('bending') of the basic word which has special grammar (e.g. past tense	*dogs* is an inflection of *dog*. *went* is an inflection of *go*. *better* is an inflection of *good*.

Term	Guidance	Example
	or plural). In contrast, adding -er to *walk* produces a completely different word, *walker*, which is part of the same word family. Inflection is sometimes thought of as merely a change of ending, but, in fact, some words change completely when inflected.	
intransitive verb	A verb which does not need an object in a sentence to complete its meaning is described as intransitive. See 'transitive verb'.	*We all laughed.* *We would like to stay longer, but we must leave.*
main clause	A sentence contains at least one clause which is not a subordinate clause; such a clause is a main clause. A main clause may contain any number of subordinate clauses.	*It was raining but the sun was shining.* [two main clauses] *The man **who wrote it** told me **that it was true**.* [one main clause containing two subordinate clauses.] *She said, "It rained all day."* [one main clause containing another.]
modal verb	Modal verbs are used to change the meaning of other verbs. They can express meanings such as certainty, ability, or obligation. The main modal verbs are *will, would, can, could, may, might, shall, should, must* and *ought*. A modal verb only has finite forms and has no suffixes (e.g. *I sing – he sings*, but not *I must – he musts*).	*I can do this maths work by myself.* *This ride may be too scary for you!* *You should help your little brother.* *Is it going to rain? Yes, it might.* *Canning swim is important.* [not possible because *can* must be finite; contrast: *Being able to swim is important*, where *being* is not a modal verb]
modify, modifier	One word or phrase modifies another by making its meaning more specific. Because the two words make a phrase, the 'modifier' is normally close to the modified word.	In the phrase *primary-school teacher*: ▪ *teacher* is modified by *primary-school* (to mean a specific kind of teacher) ▪ *school* is modified by *primary* (to mean a specific kind of school).
morphology	A word's morphology is its internal make-up in terms of root words and suffixes or prefixes, as well as other kinds of change such as the change	*dogs* has the morphological make-up: *dog + s*. *unhelpfulness* has the

Term	Guidance	Example
	of *mouse* to *mice*. Morphology may be used to produce different inflections of the same word (e.g. *boy – boys*), or entirely new words (e.g. *boy – boyish*) belonging to the same word family. A word that contains two or more root words is a compound (e.g. *news+paper, ice+cream*).	morphological make-up: *unhelpful + ness* ▪ where *unhelpful = un + helpful* ▪ and *helpful = help + ful*
noun	The surest way to identify nouns is by the ways they can be used after determiners such as *the*: for example, most nouns will fit into the frame "The __ matters/matter." Nouns are sometimes called 'naming words' because they name people, places and 'things'; this is often true, but it doesn't help to distinguish nouns from other word classes. For example, prepositions can name places and verbs can name 'things' such as actions. Nouns may be classified as **common** (e.g. *boy, day*) or **proper** (e.g. *Ivan, Wednesday*), and also as **countable** (e.g. *thing, boy*) or **non-countable** (e.g. *stuff, money*). These classes can be recognised by the determiners they combine with.	*Our dog bit the burglar on his behind!* *My big brother did an amazing jump on his skateboard.* *Actions speak louder than words.* Not nouns: ▪ *He's behind you!* [this names a place, but is a preposition, not a noun] ▪ *She can jump so high!* [this names an action, but is a verb, not a noun] common, countable: *a book, books, two chocolates, one day, fewer ideas* common, non-countable: *money, some chocolate, less imagination* proper, countable: *Marilyn, London, Wednesday*
noun phrase	A noun phrase is a phrase with a noun as its head, e.g. *some foxes, foxes with bushy tails*. Some grammarians recognise one-word phrases, so that *foxes are multiplying* would contain the noun *foxes* acting as the head of the noun phrase *foxes*.	*Adult foxes can jump.* [*adult* modifies *foxes*, so *adult* belongs to the noun phrase] *Almost all healthy adult foxes in this area can jump.* [all the other words help to modify *foxes*, so they all belong to the noun phrase]
object	An object is normally a noun, pronoun or noun phrase that comes straight after the verb, and shows what the verb is acting upon. Objects can be turned into the	*Year 2 designed puppets.* [noun acting as object] *I like that.* [pronoun acting as object]

Term	Guidance	Example
	subject of a passive verb, and cannot be adjectives (contrast with complements).	Some people suggested a pretty display. [noun phrase acting as object] Contrast: ▪ *A display was suggested.* [object of active verb becomes the subject of the passive verb] ▪ *Year 2 designed pretty.* [incorrect, because adjectives cannot be objects]
participle	Verbs in English have two participles, called 'present participle' (e.g. *walking, taking*) and 'past participle' (e.g. *walked, taken*). Unfortunately, these terms can be confusing to learners, because: ▪ they don't necessarily have anything to do with present or past time ▪ although past participles are used as perfects (e.g. *has eaten*) they are also used as passives (e.g. *was eaten*).	*He is walking to school.* [present participle in a progressive] *He has taken the bus to school.* [past participle in a perfect] *The photo was taken in the rain.* [past participle in a passive]
passive	The sentence *It was eaten by our dog* is the passive of *Our dog ate it.* A passive is recognisable from: ▪ the past participle form *eaten* ▪ the normal object (*it*) turned into the subject ▪ the normal subject (*our dog*) turned into an optional preposition phrase with *by* as its head ▪ the verb *be*(*was*), or some other verb such as *get*. Contrast active. A verb is not 'passive' just because it has a passive meaning: it must be the passive version of an active verb.	*A visit was arranged by the school.* *Our cat got run over by a bus.* Active versions: ▪ *The school arranged a visit.* ▪ *A bus ran over our cat.* Not passive: ▪ *He received a warning.* [past tense, active *received*] ▪ *We had an accident.* [past tense, active *had*]
past tense	Verbs in the past tense are commonly used to:	*Tom and Chris showed me their new TV.* [names an event in the

Term	Guidance	Example
	<ul><li>talk about the past</li><li>talk about imagined situations</li><li>make a request sound more polite.</li></ul> Most verbs take a <u>suffix</u> *—ed*, to form their past tense, but many commonly-used verbs are irregular. See also <u>tense</u>.	past] *Antonio <u>went</u> on holiday to Brazil.* [names an event in the past; irregular past of *go*] *I wish I <u>had</u> a puppy.* [names an imagined situation, not a situation in the past] *I <u>was</u> hoping you'd help tomorrow.* [makes an implied request sound more polite]
perfect	The perfect form of a <u>verb</u> generally calls attention to the consequences of a prior event; for example, *he has gone to lunch* implies that he is still away, in contrast with *he went to lunch*. 'Had gone to lunch' takes a past time point (i.e. when we arrived) as its reference point and is another way of establishing time relations in a text. The perfect tense is formed by: <ul><li>turning the verb into its past <u>participle inflection</u></li><li>adding a form of the verb *have* before it.</li></ul> It can also be combined with the <u>progressive</u> (e.g. *he has been going*).	*She <u>has downloaded</u> some songs.* [present perfect; now she has some songs] *I <u>had eaten</u> lunch when you came.* [past perfect; I wasn't hungry when you came]
phoneme	A phoneme is the smallest unit of sound that signals a distinct, contrasting meaning. For example: <ul><li>/t/ contrasts with /k/ to signal the difference between *tap* and *cap*</li><li>/t/ contrasts with /l/ to signal the difference between *bought* and *ball*.</li></ul> It is this contrast in meaning that tells us there are two distinct phonemes at work. There are around 44 phonemes in English; the exact number depends on regional accents. A single	The word *cat* has three letters and three phonemes: /kæt/ The word *catch* has five letters and three phonemes: /katʃ/ The word *caught* has six letters and three phonemes: /kɔːt/

Term	Guidance	Example
	phoneme may be represented in writing by one, two, three or four letters constituting a single grapheme.	
phrase	A phrase is a group of words that are grammatically connected so that they stay together, and that expand a single word, called the 'head'. The phrase is a noun phrase if its head is a noun, a preposition phrase if its head is a preposition, and so on; but if the head is a verb, the phrase is called a clause. Phrases can be made up of other phrases.	*She waved to her mother.* [a noun phrase, with the noun *mother* as its head] *She waved to her mother.* [a preposition phrase, with the preposition *to* as its head] *She waved to her mother.* [a clause, with the verb *waved* as its head]
plural	A plural noun normally has a suffix – *s* or –*es* and means 'more than one'. There are a few nouns with different morphology in the plural (e.g. *mice, formulae*).	*dogs* [more than one dog]; *boxes* [more than one box] *mice* [more than one mouse]
possessive	A possessive can be: ▪ a noun followed by an apostrophe, with or without *s* ▪ a possessive pronoun. The relation expressed by a possessive goes well beyond ordinary ideas of 'possession'. A possessive may act as a determiner.	*Tariq's book* [Tariq has the book] *The boys' arrival* [the boys arrive] *His obituary* [the obituary is about him] *That essay is mine.* [I wrote the essay]
prefix	A prefix is added at the beginning of a word in order to turn it into another word. Contrast suffix.	*overtake, disappear*
preposition	A preposition links a following noun, pronoun or noun phrase to some other word in the sentence. Prepositions often describe locations or directions, but can describe other things, such as relations of time. Words like *before* or *since* can act either as prepositions or as conjunctions.	*Tom waved goodbye to Christy. She'll be back from Australia in two weeks.* *I haven't seen my dog since this morning.* Contrast: *I'm going, since no-one wants me here!* [conjunction: links two clauses]

Term	Guidance	Example
preposition phrase	A preposition phrase has a preposition as its head followed by a noun, pronoun or noun phrase.	He was _in bed_. I met them _after the party_.
present tense	Verbs in the present tense are commonly used to: ▪ talk about the present ▪ talk about the future. They may take a suffix –s (depending on the subject). See also tense.	Jamal _goes_ to the pool every day. [describes a habit that exists now] He _can_ swim. [describes a state that is true now] The bus _arrives_ at three. [scheduled now] My friends _are_ coming to play. [describes a plan in progress now]
progressive	The progressive (also known as the 'continuous') form of a verb generally describes events in progress. It is formed by combining the verb's present participle (e.g. _singing_) with a form of the verb _be_ (e.g. _he was singing_). The progressive can also be combined with the perfect (e.g. _he has been singing_).	Michael _is singing_ in the store room. [present progressive] Amanda _was making_ a patchwork quilt. [past progressive] Usha _had been practising_ for an hour when I called. [past perfect progressive]
pronoun	Pronouns are normally used like nouns, except that: ▪ they are grammatically more specialised ▪ it is harder to modify them In the examples, each sentence is written twice: once with nouns, and once with pronouns (underlined). Where the same thing is being talked about, the words are shown in bold.	**Amanda** waved to **Michael**. **She** waved to **him**. **John's** mother is over there. **His** mother is over there. The **visit** will be an overnight **visit**. **This** will be an overnight **visit**. **Simon** is the person: **Simon** broke it. **He** is the one **who** broke it.
punctuation	Punctuation includes any conventional features of writing other than spelling and general layout: the standard punctuation marks . , ; : ? ! - – ( ) " " ' ' , and also word-spaces, capital letters, apostrophes, paragraph breaks and bullet points. One important role of punctuation is to indicate sentence boundaries.	"I'm going out, Usha, and I won't be long," Mum said.
Received Pronunciation	Received Pronunciation (often abbreviated to RP) is an accent which is used only by a small	

Term	Guidance	Example
	minority of English speakers in England. It is not associated with any one region. Because of its regional neutrality, it is the accent which is generally shown in dictionaries in the UK (but not, of course, in the USA). RP has no special status in the national curriculum.	
register	Classroom lessons, football commentaries and novels use different registers of the same language, recognised by differences of vocabulary and grammar. Registers are 'varieties' of a language which are each tied to a range of uses, in contrast with dialects, which are tied to groups of users.	*I regret to inform you that Mr Joseph Smith has passed away.* [formal letter] *Have you heard that Joe has died?* [casual speech] *Joe falls down and dies, centre stage.* [stage direction]
relative clause	A relative clause is a special type of subordinate clause that modifies a noun. It often does this by using a relative pronoun such as *who* or *that* to refer back to that noun, though the relative pronoun *that* is often omitted. A relative clause may also be attached to a clause. In that case, the pronoun refers back to the whole clause, rather than referring back to a noun. In the examples, the relative clauses are underlined, and both the pronouns and the words they refer back to are in bold.	*That's the **boy who** lives near school.* [*who* refers back to *boy*] *The **prize that** I won was a book.* [*that* refers back to *prize*] *The **prize** I won was a book.* [the pronoun *that* is omitted] ***Tom broke the game, which annoyed Ali.*** [*which* refers back to the whole clause]
root word	Morphology breaks words down into root words, which can stand alone, and suffixes or prefixes which can't. For example, *help* is the root word for other words in its word family such as *helpful* and *helpless*, and also for its inflections such as *helping*. Compound words (e.g. *help-desk*) contain two or more root words. When looking in a dictionary, we sometimes have to look for the	*played* [the root word is *play*] *unfair* [the root word is *fair*] *football* [the root words are *foot* and *ball*]

Term	Guidance	Example
	root word (or words) of the word we are interested in.	
schwa	The name of a vowel sound that is found only in unstressed positions in English. It is the most common vowel sound in English. It is written as /ə/ in the International Phonetic Alphabet. In the English writing system, it can be written in many different ways.	/əlɒŋ/ [_a_long] /bʌtə/ [butt_er_] /dɒktə/ [doct_or_]
sentence	A sentence is a group of words which are grammatically connected to each other but not to any words outside the sentence. The form of a sentence's main clause shows whether it is being used as a statement, a question, a command or an exclamation. A sentence may consist of a single clause or it may contain several clauses held together by subordination or co-ordination. Classifying sentences as 'simple', 'complex' or 'compound' can be confusing, because a 'simple' sentence may be complicated, and a 'complex' one may be straightforward. The terms **'single-clause sentence'** and **'multi-clause sentence'** may be more helpful.	_John went to his friend's house._ _He stayed there till tea-time._ _John went to his friend's house, he stayed there till tea-time._ [This is a 'comma splice', a common error in which a comma is used where either a full stop or a semi-colon is needed to indicate the lack of any grammatical connection between the two clauses.] _You are my friend._ [statement] _Are you my friend?_ [question] _Be my friend!_ [command] _What a good friend you are!_ [exclamation] _Ali went home on his bike to his goldfish and his current library book about pets._ [single-clause sentence] _She went shopping but took back everything she had bought because she didn't like any of it._ [multi-clause sentence]
split digraph	See digraph.	
Standard English	Standard English can be recognised by the use of a very small range of forms such as _those books, I did it_ and _I wasn't doing anything_ (rather than their non-Standard equivalents); it is not limited to any particular accent. It is the variety of English which is used, with only minor	_I did it because they were not willing to undertake any more work on those houses._ [formal Standard English] _I did it cos they wouldn't do any more work on those houses._ [casual Standard English]

Term	Guidance	Example
	variation, as a major world language. Some people use Standard English all the time, in all situations from the most casual to the most formal, so it covers most registers. The aim of the national curriculum is that everyone should be able to use Standard English as needed in writing and in relatively formal speaking.	*I done it cos they wouldn't do no more work on them houses.* [casual non-Standard English]
stress	A syllable is stressed if it is pronounced more forcefully than the syllables next to it. The other syllables are unstressed.	*ab<u>ou</u>t* *<u>vi</u>sit*
subject	The subject of a verb is normally the noun, noun phrase or pronoun that names the 'do-er' or 'be-er'. The subject's normal position is: ▪ just before the verb in a statement ▪ just after the auxiliary verb, in a question. Unlike the verb's object and complement, the subject can determine the form of the verb (e.g. *I am*, *you are*).	*<u>Rula's mother</u> went out.* *<u>That</u> is uncertain.* *<u>The children</u> will study the animals.* *Will <u>the children</u> study the animals?*
subjunctive	In some languages, the inflections of a verb include a large range of special forms which are used typically in subordinate clauses, and are called 'subjunctives'. English has very few such forms and those it has tend to be used in rather formal styles.	*The school requires that all pupils <u>be</u> honest.* *The school rules demand that pupils not <u>enter</u> the gym at lunchtime.* *If Zoë <u>were</u> the class president, things would be much better.*
subordinate, subordination	A subordinate word or phrase tells us more about the meaning of the word it is subordinate to. Subordination can be thought of as an unequal relationship between a subordinate word and a main word. For example: ▪ an adjective is subordinate to the noun it modifies ▪ subjects and objects are	*<u>big</u> dogs* [*big* is subordinate to *dogs*] *<u>Big dogs</u> need <u>long walks</u>.* [*big dogs* and *long walks* are subordinate to *need*] *We can watch TV <u>when we've finished</u>.* [*when we've finished* is subordinate to *watch*]

Term	Guidance	Example
	subordinate to their verbs. Subordination is much more common than the equal relationship of co-ordination. See also subordinate clause.	
subordinate clause	A clause which is subordinate to some other part of the same sentence is a subordinate clause; for example, in *The apple that I ate was sour*, the clause *that I ate* is subordinate to *apple* (which it modifies). Subordinate clauses contrast with co-ordinate clauses as in *It was sour but looked very tasty*. (Contrast: main clause) However, clauses that are directly quoted as direct speech are not subordinate clauses.	*That's the street where Ben lives.* [relative clause; modifies *street*] *He watched her as she disappeared.* [adverbial; modifies *watched*] *What you said was very nice.* [acts as subject of *was*] *She noticed an hour had passed.* [acts as object of *noticed*] Not subordinate: *He shouted, "Look out!"*
suffix	A suffix is an 'ending', used at the end of one word to turn it into another word. Unlike root words, suffixes cannot stand on their own as a complete word. Contract prefix.	*call – called* *teach – teacher* [turns a verb into a noun] *terror – terrorise* [turns a noun into a verb] *green – greenish* [leaves word class unchanged]
syllable	A syllable sounds like a beat in a word. Syllables consist of at least one vowel, and possibly one or more consonants.	*Cat* has one syllable. *Fairy* has two syllables. *Hippopotamus* has five syllables.
synonym	Two words are synonyms if they have the same meaning, or similar meanings. Contrast antonym.	*talk – speak* *old – elderly*
tense	In English, tense is the choice between present and past verbs, which is special because it is signalled by inflections and normally indicates differences of time. In contrast, languages like French, Spanish and Italian, have three or more distinct tense forms, including	*He studies.* [present tense – present time] *He studied yesterday.* [past tense – past time] *He studies tomorrow, or else!* [present tense – future time] *He may study tomorrow.* [present

Term	Guidance	Example
	a future tense. (See also: future.) The simple tenses (present and past) may be combined in English with the perfect and progressive.	tense + infinitive – future time] He _plans_ to _study_ tomorrow. [present tense + infinitive – future time] If he _studied_ tomorrow, he'd see the difference! [past tense – imagined future] Contrast three distinct tense forms in Spanish: ▪ _Estudia._ [present tense] ▪ _Estudió._ [past tense] ▪ _Estudiará._ [future tense]
transitive verb	A transitive verb takes at least one object in a sentence to complete its meaning, in contrast to an intransitive verb, which does not.	He _loves_ Juliet. She _understands_ English grammar.
trigraph	A type of grapheme where three letters represent one phoneme.	Hi_gh_, p_ure_, pa_tch_, he_dge_
unstressed	See stressed.	
verb	The surest way to identify verbs is by the ways they can be used: they can usually have a tense, either present or past (see also future). Verbs are sometimes called 'doing words' because many verbs name an action that someone does; while this can be a way of recognising verbs, it doesn't distinguish verbs from nouns (which can also name actions). Moreover many verbs name states or feelings rather than actions. Verbs can be classified in various ways: for example, as auxiliary, or modal; as transitive or intransitive; and as states or events.	He _lives_ in Birmingham. [present tense] The teacher _wrote_ a song for the class. [past tense] He _likes_ chocolate. [present tense; not an action] He _knew_ my father. [past tense; not an action] Not verbs: ▪ The _walk_ to Halina's house will take an hour. [noun] ▪ All that _surfing_ makes Morwenna so sleepy! [noun]
vowel	A vowel is a speech sound which is produced without any closure or obstruction of the vocal tract. Vowels can form syllables by themselves, or they may combine with consonants. In the English writing system, the letters _a_, _e_, _i_, _o_, _u_ and _y_ can represent vowels.	

Term	Guidance	Example
word	A word is a unit of grammar: it can be selected and moved around relatively independently, but cannot easily be split. In punctuation, words are normally separated by word spaces. Sometimes, a sequence that appears grammatically to be two words is collapsed into a single written word, indicated with a hyphen or apostrophe (e.g. *well-built, he's*).	*headteacher* or *head teacher* [can be written with or without a space] *I'm* going out. *9.30 am*
word class	Every word belongs to a word class which summarises the ways in which it can be used in grammar. The major word classes for English are: noun, verb, adjective, adverb, preposition, determiner, pronoun, conjunction. Word classes are sometimes called 'parts of speech'.	
word family	The words in a word family are normally related to each other by a combination of morphology, grammar and meaning.	*teach – teacher* *extend – extent – extensive* *grammar – grammatical – grammarian*

Mathematics

Purpose of study

Mathematics is a creative and highly inter-connected discipline that has been developed over centuries, providing the solution to some of history's most intriguing problems. It is essential to everyday life, critical to science, technology and engineering, and necessary for financial literacy and most forms of employment. A high-quality mathematics education therefore provides a foundation for understanding the world, the ability to reason mathematically, an appreciation of the beauty and power of mathematics, and a sense of enjoyment and curiosity about the subject.

Aims

The national curriculum for mathematics aims to ensure that all pupils:

- become **fluent** in the fundamentals of mathematics, including through varied and frequent practice with increasingly complex problems over time, so that pupils develop conceptual understanding and the ability to recall and apply knowledge rapidly and accurately.

- **reason mathematically** by following a line of enquiry, conjecturing relationships and generalisations, and developing an argument, justification or proof using mathematical language

- can **solve problems** by applying their mathematics to a variety of routine and non-routine problems with increasing sophistication, including breaking down problems into a series of simpler steps and persevering in seeking solutions.

Mathematics is an interconnected subject in which pupils need to be able to move fluently between representations of mathematical ideas. The programme of study for key stage 3 is organised into apparently distinct domains, but pupils should build on key stage 2 and connections across mathematical ideas to develop fluency, mathematical reasoning and competence in solving increasingly sophisticated problems. They should also apply their mathematical knowledge in science, geography, computing and other subjects.

Decisions about progression should be based on the security of pupils' understanding and their readiness to progress to the next stage. Pupils who grasp concepts rapidly should be challenged through being offered rich and sophisticated problems before any acceleration through new content in preparation for key stage 4. Those who are not sufficiently fluent should consolidate their understanding, including through additional practice, before moving on.

Information and communication technology (ICT)

Calculators should not be used as a substitute for good written and mental arithmetic. In secondary schools, teachers should use their judgement about when ICT tools should be used.

Spoken language

The national curriculum for mathematics reflects the importance of spoken language in pupils' development across the whole curriculum – cognitively, socially and linguistically. The quality and variety of language that pupils hear and speak are key factors in developing their mathematical vocabulary and presenting a mathematical justification, argument or proof. They must be assisted in making their thinking clear to themselves as well as others and teachers should ensure that pupils build secure foundations by using discussion to probe and remedy their misconceptions.

Attainment targets

By the end of key stage 3, pupils are expected to know, apply and understand the matters, skills and processes specified in the relevant programme of study.

Schools are not required by law to teach the example content in [square brackets] or the content indicated as being 'non-statutory'.

Key stage 3

Working mathematically

Through the mathematics content, pupils should be taught to:

Develop fluency

- consolidate their numerical and mathematical capability from key stage 2 and extend their understanding of the number system and place value to include decimals, fractions, powers and roots

- select and use appropriate calculation strategies to solve increasingly complex problems

- use algebra to generalise the structure of arithmetic, including to formulate mathematical relationships

- substitute values in expressions, rearrange and simplify expressions, and solve equations

- move freely between different numerical, algebraic, graphical and diagrammatic representations [for example, equivalent fractions, fractions and decimals, and equations and graphs]

- develop algebraic and graphical fluency, including understanding linear and simple quadratic functions

- use language and properties precisely to analyse numbers, algebraic expressions, 2-D and 3-D shapes, probability and statistics.

Reason mathematically

- extend their understanding of the number system; make connections between number relationships, and their algebraic and graphical representations

- extend and formalise their knowledge of ratio and proportion in working with measures and geometry, and in formulating proportional relations algebraically

- identify variables and express relations between variables algebraically and graphically

- make and test conjectures about patterns and relationships; look for proofs or counter-examples

- begin to reason deductively in geometry, number and algebra, including using geometrical constructions

- interpret when the structure of a numerical problem requires additive, multiplicative or proportional reasoning

- explore what can and cannot be inferred in statistical and probabilistic settings, and begin to express their arguments formally.

Solve problems

- develop their mathematical knowledge, in part through solving problems and evaluating the outcomes, including multi-step problems

- develop their use of formal mathematical knowledge to interpret and solve problems, including in financial mathematics

- begin to model situations mathematically and express the results using a range of formal mathematical representations

- select appropriate concepts, methods and techniques to apply to unfamiliar and non-routine problems.

Subject content

Number

Pupils should be taught to:

- understand and use place value for decimals, measures and integers of any size

- order positive and negative integers, decimals and fractions; use the number line as a model for ordering of the real numbers; use the symbols $=, \neq, <, >, \leq, \geq$

- use the concepts and vocabulary of prime numbers, factors (or divisors), multiples, common factors, common multiples, highest common factor, lowest common multiple, prime factorisation, including using product notation and the unique factorisation property

- use the four operations, including formal written methods, applied to integers, decimals, proper and improper fractions, and mixed numbers, all both positive and negative

- use conventional notation for the priority of operations, including brackets, powers, roots and reciprocals

- recognise and use relationships between operations including inverse operations

- use integer powers and associated real roots (square, cube and higher), recognise powers of 2, 3, 4, 5 and distinguish between exact representations of roots and their decimal approximations

- interpret and compare numbers in standard form $A \times 10^n$ $1 \leq A < 10$, where n is a positive or negative integer or zero

- work interchangeably with terminating decimals and their corresponding fractions (such as 3.5 and $\frac{7}{2}$ or 0.375 and $\frac{3}{8}$)

- define percentage as 'number of parts per hundred', interpret percentages and percentage changes as a fraction or a decimal, interpret these multiplicatively, express one quantity as a percentage of another, compare two quantities using percentages, and work with percentages greater than 100%

- interpret fractions and percentages as operators

- use standard units of mass, length, time, money and other measures, including with decimal quantities

- round numbers and measures to an appropriate degree of accuracy [for example, to a number of decimal places or significant figures]

- use approximation through rounding to estimate answers and calculate possible resulting errors expressed using inequality notation $a<x\leq b$

- use a calculator and other technologies to calculate results accurately and then interpret them appropriately

- appreciate the infinite nature of the sets of integers, real and rational numbers.

Algebra

Pupils should be taught to:

- use and interpret algebraic notation, including:
    - ab in place of $a \times b$
    - $3y$ in place of $y + y + y$ and $3 \times y$
    - a^2 in place of $a \times a$, a^3 in place of $a \times a \times a$; a^2b in place of $a \times a \times b$
    - $\frac{a}{b}$ in place of $a \div b$
    - coefficients written as fractions rather than as decimals
    - brackets

- substitute numerical values into formulae and expressions, including scientific formulae

- understand and use the concepts and vocabulary of expressions, equations, inequalities, terms and factors

- simplify and manipulate algebraic expressions to maintain equivalence by:
    - collecting like terms
    - multiplying a single term over a bracket
    - taking out common factors
    - expanding products of two or more binomials

- understand and use standard mathematical formulae; rearrange formulae to change the subject

- model situations or procedures by translating them into algebraic expressions or formulae and by using graphs

- use algebraic methods to solve linear equations in one variable (including all forms that require rearrangement)

- work with coordinates in all four quadrants

- recognise, sketch and produce graphs of linear and quadratic functions of one variable with appropriate scaling, using equations in x and y and the Cartesian plane

- interpret mathematical relationships both algebraically and graphically

- reduce a given linear equation in two variables to the standard form $y = mx + c$; calculate and interpret gradients and intercepts of graphs of such linear equations numerically, graphically and algebraically

- use linear and quadratic graphs to estimate values of y for given values of x and vice versa and to find approximate solutions of simultaneous linear equations

- find approximate solutions to contextual problems from given graphs of a variety of functions, including piece-wise linear, exponential and reciprocal graphs

- generate terms of a sequence from either a term-to-term or a position-to-term rule

- recognise arithmetic sequences and find the nth term

- recognise geometric sequences and appreciate other sequences that arise.

Ratio, proportion and rates of change

Pupils should be taught to:

- change freely between related standard units [for example time, length, area, volume/capacity, mass]

- use scale factors, scale diagrams and maps

- express one quantity as a fraction of another, where the fraction is less than 1 and greater than 1

- use ratio notation, including reduction to simplest form

- divide a given quantity into two parts in a given part:part or part:whole ratio; express the division of a quantity into two parts as a ratio

- understand that a multiplicative relationship between two quantities can be expressed as a ratio or a fraction

- relate the language of ratios and the associated calculations to the arithmetic of fractions and to linear functions

- solve problems involving percentage change, including: percentage increase, decrease and original value problems and simple interest in financial mathematics

- solve problems involving direct and inverse proportion, including graphical and algebraic representations

- use compound units such as speed, unit pricing and density to solve problems.

Geometry and measures

Pupils should be taught to:

- derive and apply formulae to calculate and solve problems involving: perimeter and area of triangles, parallelograms, trapezia, volume of cuboids (including cubes) and other prisms (including cylinders)
- calculate and solve problems involving: perimeters of 2-D shapes (including circles), areas of circles and composite shapes
- draw and measure line segments and angles in geometric figures, including interpreting scale drawings
- derive and use the standard ruler and compass constructions (perpendicular bisector of a line segment, constructing a perpendicular to a given line from/at a given point, bisecting a given angle); recognise and use the perpendicular distance from a point to a line as the shortest distance to the line
- describe, sketch and draw using conventional terms and notations: points, lines, parallel lines, perpendicular lines, right angles, regular polygons, and other polygons that are reflectively and rotationally symmetric
- use the standard conventions for labelling the sides and angles of triangle ABC, and know and use the criteria for congruence of triangles
- derive and illustrate properties of triangles, quadrilaterals, circles, and other plane figures [for example, equal lengths and angles] using appropriate language and technologies
- identify properties of, and describe the results of, translations, rotations and reflections applied to given figures
- identify and construct congruent triangles, and construct similar shapes by enlargement, with and without coordinate grids
- apply the properties of angles at a point, angles at a point on a straight line, vertically opposite angles
- understand and use the relationship between parallel lines and alternate and corresponding angles
- derive and use the sum of angles in a triangle and use it to deduce the angle sum in any polygon, and to derive properties of regular polygons
- apply angle facts, triangle congruence, similarity and properties of quadrilaterals to derive results about angles and sides, including Pythagoras' Theorem, and use known results to obtain simple proofs
- use Pythagoras' Theorem and trigonometric ratios in similar triangles to solve problems involving right-angled triangles
- use the properties of faces, surfaces, edges and vertices of cubes, cuboids, prisms, cylinders, pyramids, cones and spheres to solve problems in 3-D
- interpret mathematical relationships both algebraically and geometrically.

Probability

Pupils should be taught to:

- record, describe and analyse the frequency of outcomes of simple probability experiments involving randomness, fairness, equally and unequally likely outcomes, using appropriate language and the 0-1 probability scale

- understand that the probabilities of all possible outcomes sum to 1

- enumerate sets and unions/intersections of sets systematically, using tables, grids and Venn diagrams

- generate theoretical sample spaces for single and combined events with equally likely, mutually exclusive outcomes and use these to calculate theoretical probabilities.

Statistics

Pupils should be taught to:

- describe, interpret and compare observed distributions of a single variable through: appropriate graphical representation involving discrete, continuous and grouped data; and appropriate measures of central tendency (mean, mode, median) and spread (range, consideration of outliers)

- construct and interpret appropriate tables, charts, and diagrams, including frequency tables, bar charts, pie charts, and pictograms for categorical data, and vertical line (or bar) charts for ungrouped and grouped numerical data

- describe simple mathematical relationships between two variables (bivariate data) in observational and experimental contexts and illustrate using scatter graphs.

Science

Purpose of study

A high-quality science education provides the foundations for understanding the world through the specific disciplines of biology, chemistry and physics. Science has changed our lives and is vital to the world's future prosperity, and all pupils should be taught essential aspects of the knowledge, methods, processes and uses of science. Through building up a body of key foundational knowledge and concepts, pupils should be encouraged to recognise the power of rational explanation and develop a sense of excitement and curiosity about natural phenomena. They should be encouraged to understand how science can be used to explain what is occurring, predict how things will behave, and analyse causes.

Aims

The national curriculum for science aims to ensure that all pupils:

- develop **scientific knowledge and conceptual understanding** through the specific disciplines of biology, chemistry and physics

- develop understanding of the **nature, processes and methods of science** through different types of science enquiries that help them to answer scientific questions about the world around them

- are equipped with the scientific knowledge required to understand the **uses and implications** of science, today and for the future.

Scientific knowledge and conceptual understanding

The programmes of study describe a sequence of knowledge and concepts. While it is important that pupils make progress, it is also vitally important that they develop secure understanding of each key block of knowledge and concepts in order to progress to the next stage. Insecure, superficial understanding will not allow genuine progression: pupils may struggle at key points of transition (such as between primary and secondary school), build up serious misconceptions, and/or have significant difficulties in understanding higher-order content.

Pupils should be able to describe associated processes and key characteristics in common language, but they should also be familiar with, and use, technical terminology accurately and precisely. They should build up an extended specialist vocabulary. They should also apply their mathematical knowledge to their understanding of science, including collecting, presenting and analysing data. The social and economic implications of science are important but, generally, they are taught most appropriately within the wider school curriculum: teachers will wish to use different contexts to maximise their pupils' engagement with and motivation to study science.

The principal focus of science teaching in key stage 3 is to develop a deeper understanding of a range of scientific ideas in the subject disciplines of biology, chemistry and physics. Pupils should begin to see the connections between these subject areas and become aware of some of the big ideas underpinning scientific knowledge and understanding. Examples of these big ideas are the links between structure and function in living organisms, the particulate model as the key to understanding the properties and interactions of matter in all its forms, and the resources and means of transfer of energy as key determinants of all of these interactions. They should be encouraged to relate scientific explanations to phenomena in the world around them and start to use modelling and abstract ideas to develop and evaluate explanations.

Pupils should understand that science is about working objectively, modifying explanations to take account of new evidence and ideas and subjecting results to peer review. Pupils should decide on the appropriate type of scientific enquiry to undertake to answer their own questions and develop a deeper understanding of factors to be taken into account when collecting, recording and processing data. They should evaluate their results and identify further questions arising from them.

'Working scientifically' is described separately at the beginning of the programme of study, but must always be taught through and clearly related to substantive science content in the programme of study. Teachers should feel free to choose examples that serve a variety of purposes, from showing how scientific ideas have developed historically to reflecting modern developments in science.

Pupils should develop their use of scientific vocabulary, including the use of scientific nomenclature and units and mathematical representations.

Spoken language

The national curriculum for science reflects the importance of spoken language in pupils' development across the whole curriculum – cognitively, socially and linguistically. The quality and variety of language that pupils hear and speak are key factors in developing their scientific vocabulary and articulating scientific concepts clearly and precisely. They must be assisted in making their thinking clear, both to themselves and others, and teachers should ensure that pupils build secure foundations by using discussion to probe and remedy their misconceptions.

Attainment targets

By the end of key stage 3, pupils are expected to know, apply and understand the matters, skills and processes specified in the relevant programme of study.

Key stage 3

Working scientifically

Through the content across all three disciplines, pupils should be taught to:

Scientific attitudes

- pay attention to objectivity and concern for accuracy, precision, repeatability and reproducibility

- understand that scientific methods and theories develop as earlier explanations are modified to take account of new evidence and ideas, together with the importance of publishing results and peer review

- evaluate risks.

Experimental skills and investigations

- ask questions and develop a line of enquiry based on observations of the real world, alongside prior knowledge and experience

- make predictions using scientific knowledge and understanding

- select, plan and carry out the most appropriate types of scientific enquiries to test predictions, including identifying independent, dependent and control variables, where appropriate

- use appropriate techniques, apparatus, and materials during fieldwork and laboratory work, paying attention to health and safety

- make and record observations and measurements using a range of methods for different investigations; and evaluate the reliability of methods and suggest possible improvements

- apply sampling techniques.

Analysis and evaluation

- apply mathematical concepts and calculate results

- present observations and data using appropriate methods, including tables and graphs

- interpret observations and data, including identifying patterns and using observations, measurements and data to draw conclusions

- present reasoned explanations, including explaining data in relation to predictions and hypotheses

- evaluate data, showing awareness of potential sources of random and systematic error

- identify further questions arising from their results.

Measurement

- understand and use SI units and IUPAC (International Union of Pure and Applied Chemistry) chemical nomenclature

- use and derive simple equations and carry out appropriate calculations

- undertake basic data analysis including simple statistical techniques.

Subject content – Biology

Pupils should be taught about:

Structure and function of living organisms

Cells and organisation

- cells as the fundamental unit of living organisms, including how to observe, interpret and record cell structure using a light microscope

- the functions of the cell wall, cell membrane, cytoplasm, nucleus, vacuole, mitochondria and chloroplasts

- the similarities and differences between plant and animal cells

- the role of diffusion in the movement of materials in and between cells

- the structural adaptations of some unicellular organisms

- the hierarchical organisation of multicellular organisms: from cells to tissues to organs to systems to organisms.

The skeletal and muscular systems

- the structure and functions of the human skeleton, to include support, protection, movement and making blood cells

- biomechanics – the interaction between skeleton and muscles, including the measurement of force exerted by different muscles

- the function of muscles and examples of antagonistic muscles.

Nutrition and digestion

- content of a healthy human diet: carbohydrates, lipids (fats and oils), proteins, vitamins, minerals, dietary fibre and water, and why each is needed

- calculations of energy requirements in a healthy daily diet

- the consequences of imbalances in the diet, including obesity, starvation and deficiency diseases

- the tissues and organs of the human digestive system, including adaptations to function and how the digestive system digests food (enzymes simply as biological catalysts)

- the importance of bacteria in the human digestive system

- plants making carbohydrates in their leaves by photosynthesis and gaining mineral nutrients and water from the soil via their roots.

Gas exchange systems

- the structure and functions of the gas exchange system in humans, including adaptations to function

- the mechanism of breathing to move air in and out of the lungs, using a pressure model to explain the movement of gases, including simple measurements of lung volume

- the impact of exercise, asthma and smoking on the human gas exchange system

- the role of leaf stomata in gas exchange in plants.

Reproduction

- reproduction in humans (as an example of a mammal), including the structure and function of the male and female reproductive systems, menstrual cycle (without details of hormones), gametes, fertilisation, gestation and birth, to include the effect of maternal lifestyle on the foetus through the placenta

- reproduction in plants, including flower structure, wind and insect pollination, fertilisation, seed and fruit formation and dispersal, including quantitative investigation of some dispersal mechanisms.

Health

- the effects of recreational drugs (including substance misuse) on behaviour, health and life processes.

Material cycles and energy

Photosynthesis

- the reactants in, and products of, photosynthesis, and a word summary for photosynthesis

- the dependence of almost all life on Earth on the ability of photosynthetic organisms, such as plants and algae, to use sunlight in photosynthesis to build organic molecules that are an essential energy store and to maintain levels of oxygen and carbon dioxide in the atmosphere

- the adaptations of leaves for photosynthesis.

Cellular respiration

- aerobic and anaerobic respiration in living organisms, including the breakdown of organic molecules to enable all the other chemical processes necessary for life

- a word summary for aerobic respiration

- the process of anaerobic respiration in humans and micro-organisms, including fermentation, and a word summary for anaerobic respiration

- the differences between aerobic and anaerobic respiration in terms of the reactants, the products formed and the implications for the organism.

Interactions and interdependencies

Relationships in an ecosystem

- the interdependence of organisms in an ecosystem, including food webs and insect pollinated crops

- the importance of plant reproduction through insect pollination in human food security

- how organisms affect, and are affected by, their environment, including the accumulation of toxic materials.

Genetics and evolution

Inheritance, chromosomes, DNA and genes

- heredity as the process by which genetic information is transmitted from one generation to the next

- a simple model of chromosomes, genes and DNA in heredity, including the part played by Watson, Crick, Wilkins and Franklin in the development of the DNA model

- differences between species

- the variation between individuals within a species being continuous or discontinuous, to include measurement and graphical representation of variation

- the variation between species and between individuals of the same species means some organisms compete more successfully, which can drive natural selection

- changes in the environment may leave individuals within a species, and some entire species, less well adapted to compete successfully and reproduce, which in turn may lead to extinction

- the importance of maintaining biodiversity and the use of gene banks to preserve hereditary material.

Subject content – Chemistry

Pupils should be taught about:

The particulate nature of matter

- the properties of the different states of matter (solid, liquid and gas) in terms of the particle model, including gas pressure

- changes of state in terms of the particle model.

Atoms, elements and compounds

- a simple (Dalton) atomic model

- differences between atoms, elements and compounds

- chemical symbols and formulae for elements and compounds

- conservation of mass changes of state and chemical reactions.

Pure and impure substances

- the concept of a pure substance

- mixtures, including dissolving

- diffusion in terms of the particle model

- simple techniques for separating mixtures: filtration, evaporation, distillation and chromatography

- the identification of pure substances.

Chemical reactions

- chemical reactions as the rearrangement of atoms

- representing chemical reactions using formulae and using equations

- combustion, thermal decomposition, oxidation and displacement reactions

- defining acids and alkalis in terms of neutralisation reactions

- the pH scale for measuring acidity/alkalinity; and indicators

- reactions of acids with metals to produce a salt plus hydrogen

- reactions of acids with alkalis to produce a salt plus water

- what catalysts do.

Energetics

- energy changes on changes of state (qualitative)

- exothermic and endothermic chemical reactions (qualitative).

The Periodic Table

- the varying physical and chemical properties of different elements
- the principles underpinning the Mendeleev Periodic Table
- the Periodic Table: periods and groups; metals and non-metals
- how patterns in reactions can be predicted with reference to the Periodic Table
- the properties of metals and non-metals
- the chemical properties of metal and non-metal oxides with respect to acidity.

Materials

- the order of metals and carbon in the reactivity series
- the use of carbon in obtaining metals from metal oxides
- properties of ceramics, polymers and composites (qualitative).

Earth and atmosphere

- the composition of the Earth
- the structure of the Earth
- the rock cycle and the formation of igneous, sedimentary and metamorphic rocks
- Earth as a source of limited resources and the efficacy of recycling
- the carbon cycle
- the composition of the atmosphere
- the production of carbon dioxide by human activity and the impact on climate.

Subject content – Physics

Pupils should be taught about:

Energy

Calculation of fuel uses and costs in the domestic context

- comparing energy values of different foods (from labels) (kJ)
- comparing power ratings of appliances in watts (W, kW)
- comparing amounts of energy transferred (J, kJ, kW hour)
- domestic fuel bills, fuel use and costs
- fuels and energy resources.

Energy changes and transfers

- simple machines give bigger force but at the expense of smaller movement (and vice versa): product of force and displacement unchanged

- heating and thermal equilibrium: temperature difference between two objects leading to energy transfer from the hotter to the cooler one, through contact (conduction) or radiation; such transfers tending to reduce the temperature difference: use of insulators

- other processes that involve energy transfer: changing motion, dropping an object, completing an electrical circuit, stretching a spring, metabolism of food, burning fuels.

Changes in systems

- energy as a quantity that can be quantified and calculated; the total energy has the same value before and after a change

- comparing the starting with the final conditions of a system and describing increases and decreases in the amounts of energy associated with movements, temperatures, changes in positions in a field, in elastic distortions and in chemical compositions

- using physical processes and mechanisms, rather than energy, to explain the intermediate steps that bring about such changes.

Motion and forces

Describing motion

- speed and the quantitative relationship between average speed, distance and time (speed = distance ÷ time)

- the representation of a journey on a distance-time graph

- relative motion: trains and cars passing one another.

Forces

- forces as pushes or pulls, arising from the interaction between two objects

- using force arrows in diagrams, adding forces in one dimension, balanced and unbalanced forces

- moment as the turning effect of a force

- forces: associated with deforming objects; stretching and squashing – springs; with rubbing and friction between surfaces, with pushing things out of the way; resistance to motion of air and water

- forces measured in newtons, measurements of stretch or compression as force is changed

- force-extension linear relation; Hooke's Law as a special case

- work done and energy changes on deformation

- non-contact forces: gravity forces acting at a distance on Earth and in space, forces between magnets and forces due to static electricity.

Pressure in fluids

- atmospheric pressure, decreases with increase of height as weight of air above decreases with height

- pressure in liquids, increasing with depth; upthrust effects, floating and sinking

- pressure measured by ratio of force over area – acting normal to any surface.

Balanced forces

- opposing forces and equilibrium: weight held by stretched spring or supported on a compressed surface.

Forces and motion

- forces being needed to cause objects to stop or start moving, or to change their speed or direction of motion (qualitative only)

- change depending on direction of force and its size.

Waves

Observed waves

- waves on water as undulations which travel through water with transverse motion; these waves can be reflected, and add or cancel – superposition.

Sound waves

- frequencies of sound waves, measured in hertz (Hz); echoes, reflection and absorption of sound

- sound needs a medium to travel, the speed of sound in air, in water, in solids

- sound produced by vibrations of objects, in loud speakers, detected by their effects on microphone diaphragm and the ear drum; sound waves are longitudinal

- auditory range of humans and animals.

Energy and waves

- pressure waves transferring energy; use for cleaning and physiotherapy by ultra-sound; waves transferring information for conversion to electrical signals by microphone.

Light waves

- the similarities and differences between light waves and waves in matter

- light waves travelling through a vacuum; speed of light

- the transmission of light through materials: absorption, diffuse scattering and specular reflection at a surface

- use of ray model to explain imaging in mirrors, the pinhole camera, the refraction of light and action of convex lens in focusing (qualitative); the human eye

- light transferring energy from source to absorber leading to chemical and electrical effects; photo-sensitive material in the retina and in cameras

- colours and the different frequencies of light, white light and prisms (qualitative only); differential colour effects in absorption and diffuse reflection.

Electricity and electromagnetism

Current electricity
- electric current, measured in amperes, in circuits, series and parallel circuits, currents add where branches meet and current as flow of charge

- potential difference, measured in volts, battery and bulb ratings; resistance, measured in ohms, as the ratio of potential difference (p.d.) to current

- differences in resistance between conducting and insulating components (quantitative).

Static electricity
- separation of positive or negative charges when objects are rubbed together: transfer of electrons, forces between charged objects

- the idea of electric field, forces acting across the space between objects not in contact.

Magnetism
- magnetic poles, attraction and repulsion

- magnetic fields by plotting with compass, representation by field lines

- Earth's magnetism, compass and navigation

- the magnetic effect of a current, electromagnets, D.C. motors (principles only).

Matter

Physical changes
- conservation of material and of mass, and reversibility, in melting, freezing, evaporation, sublimation, condensation, dissolving

- similarities and differences, including density differences, between solids, liquids and gases

- Brownian motion in gases

- diffusion in liquids and gases driven by differences in concentration

- the difference between chemical and physical changes.

Particle model

- the differences in arrangements, in motion and in closeness of particles explaining changes of state, shape and density, the anomaly of ice-water transition

- atoms and molecules as particles.

Energy in matter

- changes with temperature in motion and spacing of particles

- internal energy stored in materials.

Space physics

- gravity force, weight = mass x gravitational field strength (g), on Earth g=10 N/kg, different on other planets and stars; gravity forces between Earth and Moon, and between Earth and Sun (qualitative only)

- our Sun as a star, other stars in our galaxy, other galaxies

- the seasons and the Earth's tilt, day length at different times of year, in different hemispheres

- the light year as a unit of astronomical distance.

Art and design

Purpose of study

Art, craft and design embody some of the highest forms of human creativity. A high-quality art and design education should engage, inspire and challenge pupils, equipping them with the knowledge and skills to experiment, invent and create their own works of art, craft and design. As pupils progress, they should be able to think critically and develop a more rigorous understanding of art and design. They should also know how art and design both reflect and shape our history, and contribute to the culture, creativity and wealth of our nation.

Aims

The national curriculum for art and design aims to ensure that all pupils:

- produce creative work, exploring their ideas and recording their experiences

- become proficient in drawing, painting, sculpture and other art, craft and design techniques

- evaluate and analyse creative works using the language of art, craft and design

- know about great artists, craft makers and designers, and understand the historical and cultural development of their art forms.

Attainment targets

By the end of key stage 3, pupils are expected to know, apply and understand the matters, skills and processes specified in the programme of study.

Subject content

Key stage 3

Pupils should be taught to develop their creativity and ideas, and increase proficiency in their execution. They should develop a critical understanding of artists, architects and designers, expressing reasoned judgements that can inform their own work.

Pupils should be taught:

- to use a range of techniques to record their observations in sketchbooks, journals and other media as a basis for exploring their ideas

- to use a range of techniques and media, including painting

- to increase their proficiency in the handling of different materials

- to analyse and evaluate their own work, and that of others, in order to strengthen the visual impact or applications of their work

- about the history of art, craft, design and architecture, including periods, styles and major movements from ancient times up to the present day.

Citizenship

Purpose of study

A high-quality citizenship education helps to provide pupils with knowledge, skills and understanding to prepare them to play a full and active part in society. In particular, citizenship education should foster pupils' keen awareness and understanding of democracy, government and how laws are made and upheld. Teaching should equip pupils with the skills and knowledge to explore political and social issues critically, to weigh evidence, debate and make reasoned arguments. It should also prepare pupils to take their place in society as responsible citizens, manage their money well and make sound financial decisions.

Aims

The national curriculum for citizenship aims to ensure that all pupils:

- acquire a sound knowledge and understanding of how the United Kingdom is governed, its political system and how citizens participate actively in its democratic systems of government

- develop a sound knowledge and understanding of the role of law and the justice system in our society and how laws are shaped and enforced

- develop an interest in, and commitment to, participation in volunteering as well as other forms of responsible activity, that they will take with them into adulthood

- are equipped with the skills to think critically and debate political questions, to enable them to manage their money on a day-to-day basis, and plan for future financial needs.

Attainment targets

By the end of each key stage, pupils are expected to know, apply and understand the matters, skills and processes specified in the relevant programme of study.

Subject content

Key stage 3

Teaching should develop pupils' understanding of democracy, government and the rights and responsibilities of citizens. Pupils should use and apply their knowledge and understanding whilst developing skills to research and interrogate evidence, debate and evaluate viewpoints, present reasoned arguments and take informed action.

Pupils should be taught about:

- the development of the political system of democratic government in the United Kingdom, including the roles of citizens, Parliament and the monarch

- the operation of Parliament, including voting and elections, and the role of political parties

- the precious liberties enjoyed by the citizens of the United Kingdom

- the nature of rules and laws and the justice system, including the role of the police and the operation of courts and tribunals

- the roles played by public institutions and voluntary groups in society, and the ways in which citizens work together to improve their communities, including opportunities to participate in school-based activities

- the functions and uses of money, the importance and practice of budgeting, and managing risk.

Key stage 4

Teaching should build on the key stage 3 programme of study to deepen pupils' understanding of democracy, government and the rights and responsibilities of citizens. Pupils should develop their skills to be able to use a range of research strategies, weigh up evidence, make persuasive arguments and substantiate their conclusions. They should experience and evaluate different ways that citizens can act together to solve problems and contribute to society.

Pupils should be taught about:

- parliamentary democracy and the key elements of the constitution of the United Kingdom, including the power of government, the role of citizens and Parliament in holding those in power to account, and the different roles of the executive, legislature and judiciary and a free press

- the different electoral systems used in and beyond the United Kingdom and actions citizens can take in democratic and electoral processes to influence decisions locally, nationally and beyond

- other systems and forms of government, both democratic and non-democratic, beyond the United Kingdom

- local, regional and international governance and the United Kingdom's relations with the rest of Europe, the Commonwealth, the United Nations and the wider world

- human rights and international law

- the legal system in the UK, different sources of law and how the law helps society deal with complex problems

- diverse national, regional, religious and ethnic identities in the United Kingdom and the need for mutual respect and understanding

- the different ways in which a citizen can contribute to the improvement of his or her community, to include the opportunity to participate actively in community volunteering, as well as other forms of responsible activity

- income and expenditure, credit and debt, insurance, savings and pensions, financial products and services, and how public money is raised and spent.

Computing

Purpose of study

A high-quality computing education equips pupils to use computational thinking and creativity to understand and change the world. Computing has deep links with mathematics, science, and design and technology, and provides insights into both natural and artificial systems. The core of computing is computer science, in which pupils are taught the principles of information and computation, how digital systems work, and how to put this knowledge to use through programming. Building on this knowledge and understanding, pupils are equipped to use information technology to create programs, systems and a range of content. Computing also ensures that pupils become digitally literate – able to use, and express themselves and develop their ideas through, information and communication technology – at a level suitable for the future workplace and as active participants in a digital world.

Aims

The national curriculum for computing aims to ensure that all pupils:

- can understand and apply the fundamental principles and concepts of computer science, including abstraction, logic, algorithms and data representation

- can analyse problems in computational terms, and have repeated practical experience of writing computer programs in order to solve such problems

- can evaluate and apply information technology, including new or unfamiliar technologies, analytically to solve problems

- are responsible, competent, confident and creative users of information and communication technology.

Attainment targets

By the end of each key stage, pupils are expected to know, apply and understand the matters, skills and processes specified in the relevant programme of study.

Schools are not required by law to teach the example content in [square brackets].

Subject content

Key stage 3

Pupils should be taught to:

- design, use and evaluate computational abstractions that model the state and behaviour of real-world problems and physical systems

- understand several key algorithms that reflect computational thinking [for example, ones for sorting and searching]; use logical reasoning to compare the utility of alternative algorithms for the same problem

- use two or more programming languages, at least one of which is textual, to solve a variety of computational problems; make appropriate use of data structures [for example, lists, tables or arrays]; design and develop modular programs that use procedures or functions

- understand simple Boolean logic [for example, AND, OR and NOT] and some of its uses in circuits and programming; understand how numbers can be represented in binary, and be able to carry out simple operations on binary numbers [for example, binary addition, and conversion between binary and decimal]

- understand the hardware and software components that make up computer systems, and how they communicate with one another and with other systems

- understand how instructions are stored and executed within a computer system; understand how data of various types (including text, sounds and pictures) can be represented and manipulated digitally, in the form of binary digits

- undertake creative projects that involve selecting, using, and combining multiple applications, preferably across a range of devices, to achieve challenging goals, including collecting and analysing data and meeting the needs of known users

- create, re-use, revise and re-purpose digital artefacts for a given audience, with attention to trustworthiness, design and usability

- understand a range of ways to use technology safely, respectfully, responsibly and securely, including protecting their online identity and privacy; recognise inappropriate content, contact and conduct and know how to report concerns.

Key stage 4

All pupils must have the opportunity to study aspects of information technology and computer science at sufficient depth to allow them to progress to higher levels of study or to a professional career.

All pupils should be taught to:

- develop their capability, creativity and knowledge in computer science, digital media and information technology

- develop and apply their analytic, problem-solving, design, and computational thinking skills

- understand how changes in technology affect safety, including new ways to protect their online privacy and identity, and how to identify and report a range of concerns.

Design and technology

Purpose of study

Design and technology is an inspiring, rigorous and practical subject. Using creativity and imagination, pupils design and make products that solve real and relevant problems within a variety of contexts, considering their own and others' needs, wants and values. They acquire a broad range of subject knowledge and draw on disciplines such as mathematics, science, engineering, computing and art. Pupils learn how to take risks, becoming resourceful, innovative, enterprising and capable citizens. Through the evaluation of past and present design and technology, they develop a critical understanding of its impact on daily life and the wider world. High-quality design and technology education makes an essential contribution to the creativity, culture, wealth and well-being of the nation.

Aims

The national curriculum for design and technology aims to ensure that all pupils:

- develop the creative, technical and practical expertise needed to perform everyday tasks confidently and to participate successfully in an increasingly technological world

- build and apply a repertoire of knowledge, understanding and skills in order to design and make high-quality prototypes and products for a wide range of users

- critique, evaluate and test their ideas and products and the work of others

- understand and apply the principles of nutrition and learn how to cook.

Attainment targets

By the end of key stage 3, pupils are expected to know, apply and understand the matters, skills and processes specified in the programme of study.

Schools are not required by law to teach the example content in [square brackets].

Subject content

Key stage 3

Through a variety of creative and practical activities, pupils should be taught the knowledge, understanding and skills needed to engage in an iterative process of designing and making. They should work in a range of domestic and local contexts [for example, the home, health, leisure and culture], and industrial contexts [for example, engineering, manufacturing, construction, food, energy, agriculture (including horticulture) and fashion].

When designing and making, pupils should be taught to:

Design

- use research and exploration, such as the study of different cultures, to identify and understand user needs

- identify and solve their own design problems and understand how to reformulate problems given to them

- develop specifications to inform the design of innovative, functional, appealing products that respond to needs in a variety of situations

- use a variety of approaches [for example, biomimicry and user-centred design], to generate creative ideas and avoid stereotypical responses

- develop and communicate design ideas using annotated sketches, detailed plans, 3-D and mathematical modelling, oral and digital presentations and computer-based tools

Make

- select from and use specialist tools, techniques, processes, equipment and machinery precisely, including computer-aided manufacture

- select from and use a wider, more complex range of materials, components and ingredients, taking into account their properties

Evaluate

- analyse the work of past and present professionals and others to develop and broaden their understanding

- investigate new and emerging technologies

- test, evaluate and refine their ideas and products against a specification, taking into account the views of intended users and other interested groups

- understand developments in design and technology, its impact on individuals, society and the environment, and the responsibilities of designers, engineers and technologists

Technical knowledge

- understand and use the properties of materials and the performance of structural elements to achieve functioning solutions

- understand how more advanced mechanical systems used in their products enable changes in movement and force

- understand how more advanced electrical and electronic systems can be powered and used in their products [for example, circuits with heat, light, sound and movement as inputs and outputs]

- apply computing and use electronics to embed intelligence in products that respond to inputs [for example, sensors], and control outputs [for example, actuators], using programmable components [for example, microcontrollers].

Cooking and nutrition

As part of their work with food, pupils should be taught how to cook and apply the principles of nutrition and healthy eating. Instilling a love of cooking in pupils will also open a door to one of the great expressions of human creativity. Learning how to cook is a crucial life skill that enables pupils to feed themselves and others affordably and well, now and in later life.

Pupils should be taught to:

Key stage 3

- understand and apply the principles of nutrition and health

- cook a repertoire of predominantly savoury dishes so that they are able to feed themselves and others a healthy and varied diet

- become competent in a range of cooking techniques [for example, selecting and preparing ingredients; using utensils and electrical equipment; applying heat in different ways; using awareness of taste, texture and smell to decide how to season dishes and combine ingredients; adapting and using their own recipes]

- understand the source, seasonality and characteristics of a broad range of ingredients.

Geography

Purpose of study

A high-quality geography education should inspire in pupils a curiosity and fascination about the world and its people that will remain with them for the rest of their lives. Teaching should equip pupils with knowledge about diverse places, people, resources and natural and human environments, together with a deep understanding of the Earth's key physical and human processes. As pupils progress, their growing knowledge about the world should help them to deepen their understanding of the interaction between physical and human processes, and of the formation and use of landscapes and environments. Geographical knowledge, understanding and skills provide the frameworks and approaches that explain how the Earth's features at different scales are shaped, interconnected and change over time.

Aims

The national curriculum for geography aims to ensure that all pupils:

- develop contextual knowledge of the location of globally significant places – both terrestrial and marine – including their defining physical and human characteristics and how these provide a geographical context for understanding the actions of processes

- understand the processes that give rise to key physical and human geographical features of the world, how these are interdependent and how they bring about spatial variation and change over time

- are competent in the geographical skills needed to:
    - collect, analyse and communicate with a range of data gathered through experiences of fieldwork that deepen their understanding of geographical processes
    - interpret a range of sources of geographical information, including maps, diagrams, globes, aerial photographs and Geographical Information Systems (GIS)
    - communicate geographical information in a variety of ways, including through maps, numerical and quantitative skills and writing at length.

Attainment targets

By the end of key stage 3, pupils are expected to know, apply and understand the matters, skills and processes specified in the programme of study.

Schools are not required by law to teach the example content in [square brackets].

Subject content

Key stage 3

Pupils should consolidate and extend their knowledge of the world's major countries and their physical and human features. They should understand how geographical processes interact to create distinctive human and physical landscapes that change over time. In doing so, they should become aware of increasingly complex geographical systems in the world around them. They should develop greater competence in using geographical knowledge, approaches and concepts [such as models and theories] and geographical skills in analysing and interpreting different data sources. In this way pupils will continue to enrich their locational knowledge and spatial and environmental understanding.

Pupils should be taught to:

Locational knowledge

- extend their locational knowledge and deepen their spatial awareness of the world's countries using maps of the world to focus on Africa, Russia, Asia (including China and India), and the Middle East, focusing on their environmental regions, including polar and hot deserts, key physical and human characteristics, countries and major cities

Place Knowledge

- understand geographical similarities, differences and links between places through the study of human and physical geography of a region within Africa, and of a region within Asia

Human and physical geography

- understand, through the use of detailed place-based exemplars at a variety of scales, the key processes in:
  - physical geography relating to: geological timescales and plate tectonics; rocks, weathering and soils; weather and climate, including the change in climate from the Ice Age to the present; and glaciation, hydrology and coasts
  - human geography relating to: population and urbanisation; international development; economic activity in the primary, secondary, tertiary and quaternary sectors; and the use of natural resources
- understand how human and physical processes interact to influence, and change landscapes, environments and the climate; and how human activity relies on effective functioning of natural systems

Geographical skills and fieldwork

- build on their knowledge of globes, maps and atlases and apply and develop this knowledge routinely in the classroom and in the field

- interpret Ordnance Survey maps in the classroom and the field, including using grid references and scale, topographical and other thematic mapping, and aerial and satellite photographs

- use Geographical Information Systems (GIS) to view, analyse and interpret places and data

- use fieldwork in contrasting locations to collect, analyse and draw conclusions from geographical data, using multiple sources of increasingly complex information.

History

Purpose of study

A high-quality history education will help pupils gain a coherent knowledge and understanding of Britain's past and that of the wider world. It should inspire pupils' curiosity to know more about the past. Teaching should equip pupils to ask perceptive questions, think critically, weigh evidence, sift arguments, and develop perspective and judgement. History helps pupils to understand the complexity of people's lives, the process of change, the diversity of societies and relationships between different groups, as well as their own identity and the challenges of their time.

Aims

The national curriculum for history aims to ensure that all pupils:

- know and understand the history of these islands as a coherent, chronological narrative, from the earliest times to the present day: how people's lives have shaped this nation and how Britain has influenced and been influenced by the wider world

- know and understand significant aspects of the history of the wider world: the nature of ancient civilisations; the expansion and dissolution of empires; characteristic features of past non-European societies; achievements and follies of mankind

- gain and deploy a historically grounded understanding of abstract terms such as 'empire', 'civilisation', 'parliament' and 'peasantry'

- understand historical concepts such as continuity and change, cause and consequence, similarity, difference and significance, and use them to make connections, draw contrasts, analyse trends, frame historically-valid questions and create their own structured accounts, including written narratives and analyses

- understand the methods of historical enquiry, including how evidence is used rigorously to make historical claims, and discern how and why contrasting arguments and interpretations of the past have been constructed

- gain historical perspective by placing their growing knowledge into different contexts, understanding the connections between local, regional, national and international history; between cultural, economic, military, political, religious and social history; and between short- and long-term timescales.

Attainment targets

By the end of key stage 3, pupils are expected to know, apply and understand the matters, skills and processes specified in the programme of study.

Schools are not required by law to teach the example content in [square brackets] or the content indicated as being 'non-statutory'.

Subject content

Key stage 3

Pupils should extend and deepen their chronologically secure knowledge and understanding of British, local and world history, so that it provides a well-informed context for wider learning. Pupils should identify significant events, make connections, draw contrasts, and analyse trends within periods and over long arcs of time. They should use historical terms and concepts in increasingly sophisticated ways. They should pursue historically valid enquiries including some they have framed themselves, and create relevant, structured and evidentially supported accounts in response. They should understand how different types of historical sources are used rigorously to make historical claims and discern how and why contrasting arguments and interpretations of the past have been constructed.

In planning to ensure the progression described above through teaching the British, local and world history outlined below, teachers should combine overview and depth studies to help pupils understand both the long arc of development and the complexity of specific aspects of the content.

Pupils should be taught about:

- the development of Church, state and society in Medieval Britain 1066-1509

> **Examples (non-statutory)**
>
> This could include:
>
> - the Norman Conquest
>
> - Christendom, the importance of religion and the Crusades
>
> - the struggle between Church and crown
>
> - Magna Carta and the emergence of Parliament
>
> - the English campaigns to conquer Wales and Scotland up to 1314
>
> - society, economy and culture: for example, feudalism, religion in daily life (parishes, monasteries, abbeys), farming, trade and towns (especially the wool trade), art, architecture and literature
>
> - the Black Death and its social and economic impact
>
> - the Peasants' Revolt
>
> - the Hundred Years War
>
> - the Wars of the Roses; Henry VII and attempts to restore stability

- the development of Church, state and society in Britain 1509-1745

> **Examples (non-statutory)**
>
> This could include:
>
> - Renaissance and Reformation in Europe
>
> - the English Reformation and Counter Reformation (Henry VIII to Mary I)
>
> - the Elizabethan religious settlement and conflict with Catholics (including Scotland, Spain and Ireland)
>
> - the first colony in America and first contact with India
>
> - the causes and events of the civil wars throughout Britain
>
> - the Interregnum (including Cromwell in Ireland)
>
> - the Restoration, 'Glorious Revolution' and power of Parliament
>
> - the Act of Union of 1707, the Hanoverian succession and the Jacobite rebellions of 1715 and 1745
>
> - society, economy and culture across the period: for example, work and leisure in town and country, religion and superstition in daily life, theatre, art, music and literature

- ideas, political power, industry and empire: Britain, 1745-1901

> **Examples (non-statutory)**
>
> This could include:
>
> - the Enlightenment in Europe and Britain, with links back to 17th-Century thinkers and scientists and the founding of the Royal Society
>
> - Britain's transatlantic slave trade: its effects and its eventual abolition
>
> - the Seven Years War and The American War of Independence
>
> - the French Revolutionary wars
>
> - Britain as the first industrial nation – the impact on society
>
> - party politics, extension of the franchise and social reform
>
> - the development of the British Empire with a depth study (for example, of India)
>
> - Ireland and Home Rule
>
> - Darwin's 'On The Origin of Species'

- challenges for Britain, Europe and the wider world 1901 to the present day

   In addition to studying the Holocaust, this could include:

> **Examples (non-statutory)**
> - women's suffrage
> - the First World War and the Peace Settlement
> - the inter-war years: the Great Depression and the rise of dictators
> - the Second World War and the wartime leadership of Winston Churchill
> - the creation of the Welfare State
> - Indian independence and end of Empire
> - social, cultural and technological change in post-war British society
> - Britain's place in the world since 1945

- a local history study

> **Examples (non-statutory)**
> - a depth study linked to one of the British areas of study listed above
> - a study over time, testing how far sites in their locality reflect aspects of national history (some sites may predate 1066)
> - a study of an aspect or site in local history dating from a period before 1066

- the study of an aspect or theme in British history that consolidates and extends pupils' chronological knowledge from before 1066

> **Examples (non-statutory)**
> - the changing nature of political power in Britain, traced through selective case studies from the Iron Age to the present
> - Britain's changing landscape from the Iron Age to the present
> - a study of an aspect of social history, such as the impact through time of the migration of people to, from and within the British Isles
> - a study in depth into a significant turning point: for example, the Neolithic Revolution

- at least one study of a significant society or issue in world history and its interconnections with other world developments [for example, Mughal India 1526-1857; China's Qing dynasty 1644-1911; Changing Russian empires c.1800-1989; USA in the 20th Century].

Languages

Purpose of study

Learning a foreign language is a liberation from insularity and provides an opening to other cultures. A high-quality languages education should foster pupils' curiosity and deepen their understanding of the world. The teaching should enable pupils to express their ideas and thoughts in another language and to understand and respond to its speakers, both in speech and in writing. It should also provide opportunities for them to communicate for practical purposes, learn new ways of thinking and read great literature in the original language. Language teaching should provide the foundation for learning further languages, equipping pupils to study and work in other countries.

Aims

The national curriculum for languages aims to ensure that all pupils:

- understand and respond to spoken and written language from a variety of authentic sources

- speak with increasing confidence, fluency and spontaneity, finding ways of communicating what they want to say, including through discussion and asking questions, and continually improving the accuracy of their pronunciation and intonation

- can write at varying length, for different purposes and audiences, using the variety of grammatical structures that they have learnt

- discover and develop an appreciation of a range of writing in the language studied.

Attainment targets

By the end of key stage 3, pupils are expected to know, apply and understand the matters, skills and processes specified in the programme of study.

Schools are not required by law to teach the example content in [square brackets].

Subject content

Key stage 3: Modern foreign language

Teaching may be of any modern foreign language and should build on the foundations of language learning laid at key stage 2, whether pupils continue with the same language or take up a new one. Teaching should focus on developing the breadth and depth of pupils' competence in listening, speaking, reading and writing, based on a sound foundation of core grammar and vocabulary. It should enable pupils to understand and communicate personal and factual information that goes beyond their immediate needs and interests, developing and justifying points of view in speech and writing, with increased spontaneity, independence and accuracy. It should provide suitable preparation for further study.

Pupils should be taught to:

Grammar and vocabulary

- identify and use tenses or other structures which convey the present, past, and future as appropriate to the language being studied
- use and manipulate a variety of key grammatical structures and patterns, including voices and moods, as appropriate
- develop and use a wide-ranging and deepening vocabulary that goes beyond their immediate needs and interests, allowing them to give and justify opinions and take part in discussion about wider issues
- use accurate grammar, spelling and punctuation.

Linguistic competence

- listen to a variety of forms of spoken language to obtain information and respond appropriately
- transcribe words and short sentences that they hear with increasing accuracy
- initiate and develop conversations, coping with unfamiliar language and unexpected responses, making use of important social conventions such as formal modes of address
- express and develop ideas clearly and with increasing accuracy, both orally and in writing
- speak coherently and confidently, with increasingly accurate pronunciation and intonation
- read and show comprehension of original and adapted materials from a range of different sources, understanding the purpose, important ideas and details, and provide an accurate English translation of short, suitable material
- read literary texts in the language [such as stories, songs, poems and letters], to stimulate ideas, develop creative expression and expand understanding of the language and culture

- write prose using an increasingly wide range of grammar and vocabulary, write creatively to express their own ideas and opinions, and translate short written text accurately into the foreign language.

Music

Purpose of study

Music is a universal language that embodies one of the highest forms of creativity. A high-quality music education should engage and inspire pupils to develop a love of music and their talent as musicians, and so increase their self-confidence, creativity and sense of achievement. As pupils progress, they should develop a critical engagement with music, allowing them to compose, and to listen with discrimination to the best in the musical canon.

Aims

The national curriculum for music aims to ensure that all pupils:

- perform, listen to, review and evaluate music across a range of historical periods, genres, styles and traditions, including the works of the great composers and musicians

- learn to sing and to use their voices, to create and compose music on their own and with others, have the opportunity to learn a musical instrument, use technology appropriately and have the opportunity to progress to the next level of musical excellence

- understand and explore how music is created, produced and communicated, including through the inter-related dimensions: pitch, duration, dynamics, tempo, timbre, texture, structure and appropriate musical notations.

Attainment targets

By the end of key stage 3, pupils are expected to know, apply and understand the matters, skills and processes specified in the programme of study.

Subject content

Key stage 3

Pupils should build on their previous knowledge and skills through performing, composing and listening. They should develop their vocal and/or instrumental fluency, accuracy and expressiveness; and understand musical structures, styles, genres and traditions, identifying the expressive use of musical dimensions. They should listen with increasing discrimination and awareness to inform their practice as musicians. They should use technologies appropriately and appreciate and understand a wide range of musical contexts and styles.

Pupils should be taught to:

- play and perform confidently in a range of solo and ensemble contexts using their voice, playing instruments musically, fluently and with accuracy and expression

- improvise and compose; and extend and develop musical ideas by drawing on a range of musical structures, styles, genres and traditions

- use staff and other relevant notations appropriately and accurately in a range of musical styles, genres and traditions

- identify and use the inter-related dimensions of music expressively and with increasing sophistication, including use of tonalities, different types of scales and other musical devices

- listen with increasing discrimination to a wide range of music from great composers and musicians

- develop a deepening understanding of the music that they perform and to which they listen, and its history.

Physical education

Purpose of study

A high-quality physical education curriculum inspires all pupils to succeed and excel in competitive sport and other physically-demanding activities. It should provide opportunities for pupils to become physically confident in a way which supports their health and fitness. Opportunities to compete in sport and other activities build character and help to embed values such as fairness and respect.

Aims

The national curriculum for physical education aims to ensure that all pupils:

- develop competence to excel in a broad range of physical activities
- are physically active for sustained periods of time
- engage in competitive sports and activities
- lead healthy, active lives.

Attainment targets

By the end of each key stage, pupils are expected to know, apply and understand the matters, skills and processes specified in the relevant programme of study.

Schools are not required by law to teach the example content in [square brackets].

Subject content

Key stage 3

Pupils should build on and embed the physical development and skills learned in key stages 1 and 2, become more competent, confident and expert in their techniques, and apply them across different sports and physical activities. They should understand what makes a performance effective and how to apply these principles to their own and others' work. They should develop the confidence and interest to get involved in exercise, sports and activities out of school and in later life, and understand and apply the long-term health benefits of physical activity.

Pupils should be taught to:

- use a range of tactics and strategies to overcome opponents in direct competition through team and individual games [for example, badminton, basketball, cricket, football, hockey, netball, rounders, rugby and tennis]

- develop their technique and improve their performance in other competitive sports [for example, athletics and gymnastics]

- perform dances using advanced dance techniques within a range of dance styles and forms

- take part in outdoor and adventurous activities which present intellectual and physical challenges and be encouraged to work in a team, building on trust and developing skills to solve problems, either individually or as a group

- analyse their performances compared to previous ones and demonstrate improvement to achieve their personal best

- take part in competitive sports and activities outside school through community links or sports clubs.

Key stage 4

Pupils should tackle complex and demanding physical activities. They should get involved in a range of activities that develops personal fitness and promotes an active, healthy lifestyle.

Pupils should be taught to:

- use and develop a variety of tactics and strategies to overcome opponents in team and individual games [for example, badminton, basketball, cricket, football, hockey, netball, rounders, rugby and tennis]

- develop their technique and improve their performance in other competitive sports,[for example, athletics and gymnastics], or other physical activities [for example, dance]

- take part in further outdoor and adventurous activities in a range of environments which present intellectual and physical challenges and which encourage pupils to work in a team, building on trust and developing skills to solve problems, either individually or as a group

- evaluate their performances compared to previous ones and demonstrate improvement across a range of physical activities to achieve their personal best

- continue to take part regularly in competitive sports and activities outside school through community links or sports clubs.